Open Skies
Eisenhower's Proposal of July 21, 1955

T0316795

Ideas and Action Series, No. 4

W. W. Rostow
Open Skies

Eisenhower's Proposal of July 21, 1955

 University of Texas Press, Austin

Copyright © 1982 by the University of Texas Press
All rights reserved
Printed in the United States of America

First Edition, 1982

Requests for permission to reproduce material from this work should be
sent to
Permissions, University of Texas Press
Box 7819
Austin, Texas 78712

Library of Congress Cataloging in Publication Data
Rostow, W. W. (Walt Whitman), 1916–
  Open skies.

  (Ideas and action series; no. 4)
  Includes bibliographical references and index.
  1. Atomic weapons and disarmament.   2. Disarmament—
Inspection.   3. United States—Foreign relations—Soviet
Union.   4. Soviet Union—Foreign relations—United
States.   I. Title.   II. Series.
JX1974.7.R58   1982   327.1'74   82-15896
ISBN 978-0-292-76024-0

In memory of
Nelson Aldrich Rockefeller

Contents

Preface

This is the fourth in a series of essays centered on the relationship between ideas and action. The first was *Pre-Invasion Bombing Strategy*; the second, *The Division of Europe after World War II: 1946*; the third, *Europe after Stalin*. Here the summit meeting, rejected by Eisenhower and Dulles in the wake of Stalin's death, at last takes place; and we examine the origins and significance of its most memorable moment: Eisenhower's presentation of the Open Skies proposal.

As for the general theme of the series, I would define ideas as the abstract concepts in the minds of public officials and their advisers which they bring to bear in making decisions. My experiences as both an academic and a public servant have equally driven home over the years this piece of wisdom from George Santayana's *Character and Opinion in the United States*:

> . . . human discourse is intrinsically addressed not to natural existing things but to ideal essences, poetic or logical terms which thought may define and play with. When fortune or necessity diverts our attention from this congenial ideal sport to crude facts and pressing issues, we turn our frail poetic ideas into symbols for those terrible irruptive things. In that paper money of our own stamping, the legal tender of the mind, we are obliged to reckon all the movements and values of the world.

But there is, of course, a good deal more to decisions in public policy than clash and choice among the "frail poetic ideas" we create to make simplified sense of an inordinately complex and usually disheveled field of action. A decision is, after all, a choice among perceived alternatives. Ideas play a large role in defining those alternatives, but the choice among them involves other factors. The precise setting and timing of the decision evidently matter. So do questions of power, that is, politics and bureaucratic vested interests. So do personalities—unique human beings, controlled by mem ories and experiences, dreams and hopes which James Gould Cozzens evoked, in *By Love Possessed*, in a definition of temperament:

> A man's temperament might, perhaps, be defined as the mode or modes of a man's feeling, the struck balance of his ruling desires, the worked-out sum of his habitual pre- dispositions. In themselves, these elements were inscrutable. There were usually too many of them; they were often of irreducible complexity; you could observe only results. . . . The to-be-observed result was a total way of life.

And, as we shall see vividly in the story told here, tempera- ments thus broadly defined sometimes clash at both the working levels and the highest reaches of government, adding a special wild card to the way history unfolds.

In this effort to illuminate the relationship between ideas and action, I decided to proceed as follows. First, to examine a series of specific decisions taken by particular high public officials at particular times and to reflect on the decision- making process as a whole in a final essay. In the case studies, the decision would be briefly described, including the op- tions which the executive perceived as available to him; the conceptual debate involved in the decision—the more or less pure intellectual content of the process—would be de- lineated; the larger background of events would be evoked;

the interplay between the conceptual debate and the other more mundane forces in play would be examined; the follow-on events and consequences of the decision would be weighed; and some larger lessons of the story would be drawn. Along the way an effort would be made to capture the odd, often adventitious circumstances which entered into the decision and into the way things actually turned out. There are strands of accident and even humor—high, low, or wry—running through a good many of these case studies as well as pratfalls from which even the highest officials are not exempt. Indeed, this is a built-in hazard of the human condition, because decisions are almost always made with imperfect information and foresight, involving a step into the dark. Unlike the first essay of this series, here we are not dealing literally with men groping through "the fog of war," but the image is equally apt for those trying simultaneously to respect the imperatives of the Cold War and to explore the possibilities of breaking out of its grip, as Eisenhower tried at Geneva.

The occasion examined here was the second major American initiative designed to bring order and security to a world shadowed by nuclear weapons. The first such effort was the presentation to the United Nations of the proposal for an International Atomic Development Authority on June 14, 1946. Eisenhower's Open Skies proposal was, of course, more modest; and it was made at a time when the United States and the U.S.S.R. were well along the road in a race to develop missiles tipped with thermonuclear weapons. Moreover, the Open Skies proposal was made in circumstances touched by the need for the United States to achieve at the summit a positive political and psychological result. It was also a time when responsible American officials were authentically frustrated and alarmed by our inability to penetrate the closed society of the U.S.S.R. and establish with reasonable precision the scale and momentum of the Soviet program to develop nuclear delivery capabilities which could mortally threaten Western Europe, Japan, and the United States. Plans were afoot at the time of the summit to deploy photographic reconnaissance vehicles over the Soviet Union, unless an agreement for mutual aerial inspection with the Soviet Union could be achieved. Nevertheless, the evidence is firm that Eisenhower viewed Open Skies, in his own phrase, as an idea that might "open a tiny gate in the disarmament fence," and there is not the slightest doubt that he took arms control very seriously indeed. An additional quarter century's experience with the task of arms control confirms that no serious agreement is possible without inspection provisions all can trust. And, with the advent of satellite photography, the Soviet government came to accept that proposition despite their asymmetrical intelligence advantage. Thus, we have, in fact, lived with Eisenhower's Open Skies proposal for twenty years.

I have chosen in this series to examine decisions in which I played some role or which I had an opportunity to observe closely at the time. But, as the reader will perceive, this and the other volumes in the series are not exercises in autobiography. It is simply the case that one has a better chance of capturing something of the relationship between ideas and the other elements determining action if one was reasonably close to events than if the whole complex setting has to be reconstructed from the beginning.

On the other hand, my memory of the circumstances, the material in my files, and my knowledge of some of the actors were patently inadequate. In this and the other case studies, my purpose is to bring to bear what public records, communication with participants, and the literature of published memoirs and works of scholarship can now provide. As in the present volume, there is usually a formidable body of relevant material available.

Certain source or other basic materials, hitherto unpublished or not easily accessible, have been assembled in the appendixes to this book. They are meant to illuminate facets of the decision examined or to capture something of the moods and temper of the time.

Dr. Ted Carpenter, a scholar of this period, has been of invaluable assistance both in mobilizing relevant primary and secondary sources and as a critic of drafts. Our work on this essay was supported by grants from the University Research Institute of the University of Texas at Austin and the National Endowment for the Humanities, whose indispensable help I wish warmly to acknowledge.

I should also like to thank the participants in these events and the scholars who have generously given their time for guidance and criticism: Robert B. Anderson, Richard M. Bissell, Jr., Robert Bowie, McGeorge Bundy, Clark Clifford, Robert A. Divine, Eleanor Lansing Dulles, John S. D. Eisenhower, Alfred Goldberg, Andrew J. Goodpaster, Fred I. Greenstein, John W. Hanes, Jr., Nancy Hanks, Richard H. Immerman, Mrs. C. D. Jackson, Stephen Jurika, William R. Kintner, Phyllis Bernau Macomber, William B. Macomber, Marie McCrum, Hugh Morrow, Alan F. Neidle, Theodore W. Parker, Robert Perry, Stefan Possony, Gary W. Reichard, Laurance S. Rockefeller, Elspeth D. Rostow, Ann Whitman, and Paul Wortham.

Our task was eased by the knowledgeable assistance of Mrs. Nancy Bressler, at the Seeley G. Mudd Manuscript Library, Princeton University, and by the archivists of the Dwight D. Eisenhower Library at Abilene who reached out to help us. I am also in the debt of Hugh Morrow for arranging access to papers personally released for publication by Nelson A. Rockefeller before his death and to J. W. F. Dulles for permission to quote from a letter by his father to C. D. Jackson (see Appendix H).

As on many other occasions, I was aided in multiple ways by Lois Nivens. Frances Knape was most helpful in typing the various drafts.

I should add that this series of essays would not have been

undertaken without the strong encouragement of my wife, Elspeth Davies Rostow, who believed I might usefully reflect on the large central question embedded in those periods in my professional life when I was diverted from strictly academic pursuits.

W. W. Rostow

April 1982
Austin, Texas

Open Skies
Eisenhower's Proposal of July 21, 1955

1. The Decision

At 6:00 P.M. on Wednesday, July 20, 1955, President Eisenhower assembled an impressive group of American public servants in the library at the Château du Creux de Genthod, an eighteenth-century villa on Lake Geneva where he stayed while attending the summit conference of July 18–23. Those present included his major national security advisers, excepting the secretary of defense and the director of Central Intelligence, who had remained in Washington: John Foster Dulles, secretary of state; Robert B. Anderson, deputy secretary of defense; Livingston Merchant, assistant secretary of state for European affairs; Arthur W. Radford, chairman of the Joint Chiefs of Staff; Harold E. Stassen, special assistant to the president on disarmament; Dillon Anderson, special assistant to the president for national security affairs; Nelson A. Rockefeller, special assistant to the president; and Andrew J. Goodpaster, White House staff secretary. Alfred M. Gruenther, Supreme Allied Commander in Europe, was also present.

With Eisenhower and Dulles side by side in easy chairs by the fireplace and the others distributed informally around the room, the subject of discussion was what the president should say the next day at the meeting with his three colleagues: Prime Minister Anthony Eden, Edgar Faure, the French premier, and Nikolai Bulganin, nominally the head of the Soviet delegation.[1] Disarmament was the scheduled subject, and it was agreed that Eisenhower would focus on the problem of mutual inspection.

The choice before Eisenhower was, essentially, this: after discussing the critical role of inspection, should he refer the issue to Stassen for negotiation elsewhere, or should he personally propose a scheme for mutual aerial inspection which had been advocated within the government by Nelson Rockefeller since June 10?

Stassen had prepared a draft statement for the president to make the next day. That statement, accounts of the July 20 meeting by Dillon Anderson and Goodpaster, and a supplementary memorandum for the record by Goodpaster are included in Appendix A. Stassen's draft statement made the case for the critical importance of inspection, recommended that the Big Four instruct their representatives in the United Nations Subcommittee on Disarmament to give priority attention to the matter, and added the following:

> The United States is ready to proceed in the study and testing of a reliable system of inspections and reporting, and when that system is proved, then to reduce armaments with all others to the extent that the system will provide assured results.
>
> The successful working out of such a system would do much to develop the mutual confidence which will open wide the avenues of progress for all our peoples.

Eisenhower's thoughts, however, were ranging well beyond Stassen's somewhat chaste bureaucratic draft and moving toward support for Rockefeller's proposal. In fact, he reported to the meeting that he had already indicated to Eden and his British colleagues at breakfast that morning that "a plan for mutual overflights in the East and the West, to include Russia and the United States, would not be unacceptable to him." Notes on the meeting with Eden are in Appendix B.

As often happens, the official minutes and memoranda for

the record are not wholly clear about the course and texture of the discussion on the evening of the twentieth. They suggest, however, that Stassen initially took the position that such schemes "would tend to fix 'the iron curtain' more firmly." Eisenhower said they would have the opposite effect. Stassen was also concerned that the ground inspections, envisaged to supplement mutual photographic coverage, might reveal "our own advanced technology." Robert Anderson said that, while lists of military installations would be furnished, "not everything would be available for examination" on the ground. Dulles thought the U.S. would be under obligation to inform the British and French before the president made any such proposal. Evidently this might make its presentation the next day difficult, if not impossible.

After statements of support from the senior military men present (Radford and Gruenther), a consensus emerged. For some six weeks Dulles and Stassen had been resisting the concept of a specific presidential initiative for mutual aerial inspection; but with Radford and Gruenther aboard, as well as the deputy secretary of defense, on what was, essentially, a military proposal, they were evidently outgunned in narrow bureaucratic terms. But the decisive fact was that Eisenhower was strongly drawn to the proposal.

Stassen then stated that the initiative by the president the next day would "constitute a splendid opening step in the move toward disarmament." Dulles proceeded to reverse his earlier position: he opined that as both "drama and substance" the proposal was "very promising" and would have a "very great effect" but that there must be no advance word to anyone. Much of the impact would be lost if a leak occurred. So far as the records show, Nelson Rockefeller did not speak at this evening meeting, but he had met with Eisenhower and Stassen in midmorning and certainly discussed the plan.

The evening meeting closed with an agreement on tactics:

> . . . it would be best for the President to make a broad and basic opening statement giving his over-all views in the mat-

ter, and then on the "second round" put forward the proposal for overflights as a specific, more or less spontaneous,
suggestion.

Eisenhower's text and tactics were refined the next morning,
but the decision to go forward with the proposal had been
made.

On Thursday afternoon, July 21, Eisenhower played out
the script, including its planned quasispontaneous passage,
with éclat. He proceeded about two-thirds through the Stassen
draft and then interjected the following:

> Gentlemen, since I have been working on this memoran-
> dum to present to this conference, I have been searching my
> heart and mind for something that I could say here that
> could convince everyone of the great sincerity of the United
> States in approaching this problem of disarmament.
>
> I should address myself for a moment principally to the
> delegates from the Soviet Union, because our two great
> countries admittedly possess new and terrible weapons in
> quantities which do give rise in other parts of the world, or
> reciprocally, to the fears and dangers of surprise attack.
>
> I propose, therefore, that we take a practical step, that we
> begin an arrangement, very quickly, as between ourselves—
> immediately. These steps would include:
>
> To give to each other a complete blueprint of our military
> establishments, from beginning to end, from one end of our
> countries to the other; lay out the establishments and pro-
> vide the blueprints to each other.
>
> Next, to provide within our countries facilities for aerial
> photography to the other country—we to provide you the
> facilities within our country, ample facilities for aerial recon-
> naissance, where you can make all the pictures you choose
> and take them to your own country to study; you to provide
> exactly the same facilities for us and we to make these
> examinations, and by this step to convince the world that
> we are providing as between ourselves against the possibility
> of great surprise attack, thus lessening danger and relaxing
> tensions.

Likewise we will make more easily attainable a comprehensive and effective system of inspection and disarmament, because what I propose, I assure you, would be but a beginning.

He then picked up the Stassen draft with its recommendation for instructing the U.N. Subcommittee on Disarmament.

Thus ended almost two months of internecine strife within the federal bureaucracy in which John Foster Dulles and Nelson Rockefeller were the central antagonists, but in which a substantial part of the regular bureaucracy concerned with national security affairs was arrayed against Rockefeller and his scheme. The various dimensions of the struggle will be outlined in Chapter 4.

As for the immediate aftermath of Eisenhower's initiative, his memoirs supply the best account:

As I finished, a most extraordinary natural phenomenon took place. Without warning, and simultaneous with my closing words, the loudest clap of thunder I have ever heard roared into the room, and the conference was plunged into Stygian darkness. Our astonishment was all the greater because in our air-conditioned and well-lighted room there had been no inkling of an approaching storm.

For a moment there was stunned silence. Then I remarked that I had not dreamed I was so eloquent as to put the lights out. This was rewarded with laughter, only because it was an obvious break in the tension, and in a few moments the lights came back on.

At once, the Prime Minister of Britain and the Premier of France spoke in highly approving terms of the proposal. They declared themselves ready to cooperate and to open their territories to aerial inspection, provided only that all present were in agreement.

Chairman Bulganin spoke last. For a time it appeared that the intransigent Soviet refusal to permit any useful inspection system in the U.S.S.R. might be effectively shaken. The proposal, Bulganin declared, seemed to have real merit, and the Soviets would give it complete and sympathetic study at once. The tone of his talk seemed as encouraging as his words and my first reaction was that the assurance of isolation of inspection teams from the populations, eliminating any possible political indoctrination by such detachments, might prove to be a lead to progress between us.

The hope born of this development was fleeting. Shortly after Premier Bulganin spoke, the session adjourned for the day, all members apparently in high good humor. As was my custom, I mingled with the Soviet delegation. We walked together to the cocktail lounge. Daily, at adjournment time, we participated in what was apparently an international substitute for the British hour of tea. On this occasion, as it happened, I walked with Mr. Khrushchev. "I don't agree with the chairman," he said, smiling—but there was no smile in his voice. I saw clearly then, for the first time, the identity of the real boss of the Soviet delegation.

From that moment until the final adjournment of the conference, I wasted no more time probing Mr. Bulganin; I devoted myself exclusively to an attempt to persuade Mr. Khrushchev of the merits of the Open Skies plan, but to no avail. He said the idea was nothing more than a bald espionage plot against the U.S.S.R., and to this line of argument he stubbornly adhered. He made his points laughingly—but his argument was definite and intractable.

Despite the apparent futility of doing so, I continued the discussion. I urged upon him the value of an effective plan in which both sides could trust. In view of his assertions that the U.S.S.R. had nothing but peaceful intentions while the NATO powers were planning aggressive war, it was greatly to his advantage, I said, to use every legitimate opportunity to keep his government informed of all NATO moves in return for giving NATO powers the same important privileges in the U.S.S.R. I told him also that we in the United States would accept the Soviet plan of fixed posts if they would accept ours of aerial inspection. His protests were, of course, spurious. Khrushchev's own purpose was evident—*at all costs to keep the U.S.S.R. a closed society*. He would permit no effective penetration of Soviet national territory or discovery of its military secrets, no matter what reciprocal opportunities were offered to him. Of course, he was aware that without agreement of any kind there was already available to the Soviet government a vast volume of information about us which was constantly being accumulated at little or no cost from United States newspapers, road maps, aerial photographs, magazines, journals, and government reports—some of it of types that could not be obtained even from aerial reconnaissance.

There was this to say for Mr. Khrushchev. As a member of a dictatorial government, protecting his country's own military and economic fabric from foreign eyes, while having available a fairly well filled-in picture of the military strength, dispositions, and capacity of others, he was, in a selfish nationalistic sense, partly right in the course he pursued. But in the same sense he was also partly wrong, for uncontrolled armaments might well lead in the long run to the destruction of his own country. Certainly for a world statesman, ostensibly concerned with the future peace and well-being of mankind, such a course would be egregiously wrong. Khrushchev, however, does not want peace, save on his own terms and in ways that will aggrandize his own power. . . . In our use of the word, he is not, therefore, a statesman, but rather a powerful, skillful, ruthless, and highly ambitious politician.[2]

Despite Khrushchev's prompt, dour, but smiling rejection, the Open Skies proposal was generally accounted a great Eisenhower success. It provided, as Dulles had predicted, drama and substance for Eisenhower's five otherwise rather barren days on the world stage; and it strongly reinforced his image as a statesman trying to lead the world toward peace.

This was not the end of the story of aerial inspection or, indeed, the beginning. At the time of the Geneva summit conference the United States was at work on a program to photograph the U.S.S.R., both from balloons and from the U-2 aircraft, then abuilding. Less urgent work was going forward on the possibilities of satellite photography.[3] The balloon program actually ran from November 1955 to the spring of 1956;

it ended presumably because the U-2 was under rapid development. The U-2 was test-flown from an American base on August 6, 1955, and made its first overflight of the Soviet Union in July 1956. Satellite photography was not attempted until February 1959 and was conducted successfully for the first time on August 18, 1960.[4] Operations were held up, in part, because appropriate rocket boosters did not become available until the end of 1957 (THOR) and late August 1958 (ATLAS).

Of those around the table at the president's villa in Geneva on July 20, 1955, Eisenhower, Dulles, Radford, and Goodpaster certainly knew of these possibilities. There is not a line I could find in the documentary records suggesting how they viewed the Open Skies proposal in relation to the U.S. intention to initiate unilaterally aerial inspection of the Soviet Union. One can assume that Eisenhower concluded the world would be better off if such aerial inspection were done by agreement and that the U.S. position would be stronger in the future with regard to unilateral aerial photography if the Open Skies offer were made before the U.S. flights over the U.S.S.R. began.

The initial upshot of the Soviet rejection of Open Skies and the U.S. proceeding with its unilateral plans was trouble. In May 1960 the shooting down of a U-2 was used by Khrushchev as the occasion to break up the summit conference in Paris. Three months later the U.S. successfully began regular satellite photography of the U.S.S.R. The Soviet Union reciprocated with KOSMOS I, launched on March 16, 1962.[5] Both sides came to accept the procedure, the Soviet Union, no doubt, after considerable uncertainty and inner debate; but, in a sense, the overflight of the United States by the first Sputnik in October 1957 tended to settle the matter. It would have been difficult for the U.S.S.R. to object to photographic satellites, having already set the precedent that overflight in space was to be regarded by other nations as acceptable.[6]

Indeed, Khrushchev acknowledged as much in the midst of the turbulent exchanges at the Paris summit meeting of May 1960, as Eisenhower reports:

> When I finished, General de Gaulle made the interesting observation that within the last few days a Soviet satellite had been passing over France and for all that the French had been told about the nature of the orbiting vehicle, reconnaissance photographs could have been made of all French territory.
>
> Khrushchev broke in to say he was talking about airplanes, not about satellites. He said any nation in the world who wanted to photograph the Soviet areas by satellite was completely free to do so.[7]

Thus the world has lived for two decades acknowledging as common law the legitimacy of a part, at least, of what Eisenhower proposed on July 21, 1955.

Before turning to the considerations which took Eisenhower to Geneva and the intellectual and other controversies which suffused the six weeks or so preceding Eisenhower's thunderclap, it is worth noting that the origins of the idea, so far as public policy was concerned, lay in concepts and proposals much broader than mutual aerial inspection. They were incorporated in the report of the Quantico Panel, June 10, 1955, an exercise organized by Rockefeller which is examined in some detail in Chapter 3. Briefly, that report argued that the United States enjoyed as of 1955 a significant military advantage over the Soviet Union. The gap was narrowing and might close by, say, 1960 if present trends continued:

> Because of the technological acceleration of the arms race and the nature of our adversary, we run the risk that he may, at some stage, achieve a technological breakthrough, and that at that time he would be prepared to exploit his advantage by initiating an attack on the United States. Or he might use his superiority for large-scale atomic blackmail, against the United States or other powers.

The Geneva summit should, therefore, be used as a test of Soviet intentions; the test should take the form of a series of proposals, each serious but representing a spectrum of degree of difficulty for the Soviet Union to accept unless its intentions were, indeed, pacific. The spectrum ranged from mutual aerial inspection and German unity to increased cultural and other East-West contacts. If it were established at the summit that the Soviet Union was interested in cooperation only at the lower range, that fact should be the signal for a much more energetic U.S. military and foreign policy, including enlarged assistance to developing countries. Only by frustrating in these ways the Soviet vision of closing the gap and, indeed, widening it to its advantage was Washington likely to persuade Moscow to undertake serious efforts toward peace as we understood it. That was the Quantico Panel's doctrine.

On Friday, July 22, Eisenhower did make a series of proposals at the lower, easier end of the spectrum, including expanded cultural exchanges and trade. But, in adopting the Open Skies initiative, there is no evidence that Eisenhower accepted the Quantico perspective as a whole. He was, of course, aware that the gap between U.S. and Soviet nuclear capabilities was narrowing. And it is difficult to reconstruct in the 1980s the anxiety and frustration felt by responsible American leaders in the 1950s at their ignorance of how far and how fast the U.S.S.R. was moving toward nuclear parity or a superiority that might lead them to a first strike.[8] That anxiety and frustration underlay the Open Skies proposal as well as the balloons, U-2, and work on satellite photography. But Eisenhower did not view the presentation of the "hard" proposals at Geneva as a test where failure had urgent consequences for U.S. national security policy.

On the other hand, Rockefeller did accept the Quantico conception; he acted on it by organizing a second Quantico meeting in September 1955 which estimated the substantial budgetary requirements for a more vigorous U.S. response to the Soviet challenge in both military hardware and policy toward the developing regions. After his proposals were rejected by Eisenhower, Rockefeller resigned to set up the Rockefeller Brothers Fund Panels, a bipartisan effort to establish a consensus in support of more effective domestic as well as foreign and military policy. In the wake of the Soviet launching of the first Sputnik, a consensus of that kind did, indeed, emerge to which the reports of the Rockefeller Panels contributed. That consensus was the basis for a good many of the Kennedy initiatives of 1961–1963. But by that time the Soviet Union had narrowed much of the gap which existed in 1955, and in the post-Sputnik period the United States was, in several dimensions, on the defensive.

The conflict over Rockefeller's views within the Eisenhower administration in 1955 involved elements that had little to do with concept and policy. Nevertheless, the conflict cannot be fully understood without an awareness of the larger issues—including budgetary issues—embedded within the matrix from which the Open Skies proposal emerged.

But, before dealing with these matters, it is necessary to explain briefly how the Geneva summit meeting came about.

2. Three Roads to Geneva: From Moscow, Western Europe, and Washington

As the third book in this series, *Europe after Stalin*, details, there was a good deal of consideration given, in Washington and elsewhere, during the spring of 1953 to the possibility of a summit meeting in the wake of Stalin's death. In effect, Churchill, who wanted an early meeting with the new Soviet rulers, was overruled by Eisenhower and Dulles, who were, no doubt, bolstered by the knowledge that Eden, as British foreign secretary, disagreed with his chief. Two years later a consensus emerged in London and Paris, Moscow and Washington that a four-power conference should be held in July. The by no means identical reasons for agreement to go to Geneva arose from strategies pursued and events that intervened in the time since Stalin passed from the scene.

So far as the Soviet Union was concerned, a phase of strategy was drawing to a close as Stalin died. For eight years Moscow had focused its external policy on maximizing the extension of Soviet power in the war-disrupted areas of Europe and Asia. Eastern Europe was consolidated, except Yugoslavia. In Asia, the Chinese mainland was under Communist rule, as was North Korea, while Communist power in Indochina was substantial. On the other hand, the nations of Western Europe, including Germany and Italy, had emerged as democratic states, had recovered remarkably, and were woven into a security structure backed by an unambiguous American commitment. The Chinese Communist forces had been badly defeated in Korea in April–May 1951; Mao was ready to turn to the tasks of his first Five-Year Plan; and there was danger that if Ho Chi Minh tried to push too far south from his northern base he might trigger American intervention—an outcome feared at the time in both Moscow and Peking.

There was an impulse, then, in the Communist world to recognize that postwar expansion in northern Eurasia had gone about as far as it could go without excessive risk and cost and to look elsewhere.

Even before Stalin's death, at the Nineteenth Party Congress of October 1952, there were intimations of a change in Soviet strategy; but only after Stalin's death did it become clear that an uneasy collective Soviet leadership was working to a new agenda. Essentially, it came to rest on three questions. How should military force be reorganized in the light of fusion weapons and the possibilities of long-range missiles? What position should be adopted toward the governments and peoples of Asia, the Middle East, Africa, and Latin America as they pressed forward to assert themselves on the world scene and to modernize their societies? In the light of these two new elements, each of which profoundly affected the status of Western Europe, what policy should be adopted toward that area?

First, the new weaponry. From the moment at Potsdam in July 1945 when Truman told a well-informed Stalin that the United States had successfully tested a nuclear weapon, the Soviet Union adopted a posture of studied poise. While work proceeded at highest pitch within the Soviet Union on nuclear weapons, Soviet military doctrine continued to rely on ground forces with tactical air support; and Stalin steadily reaffirmed the view—a mixture of the dogmas of a Communist and a Russian ground force soldier—that nuclear weapons had in no way fundamentally altered the "permanently operating factors" which determine the outcome of war: the stability of the rear, the morale of the army, the quantity and quality of divisions, the army's weapons, and the organizing ability of the commanding officers.

In diplomacy, the Soviets refused to entertain seriously any system for international control of nuclear weapons while the American monopoly held and they were at a tactical disadvantage. In psychological warfare, through peace movements and other devices, by heightening the widespread sense of horror at the destructive possibilities of the new weapons, they maintained maximum political pressure on the United States not to bring to bear its monopolistic advantage.

There was virtually no overt change in the Soviet posture between September 1949, when the first Soviet nuclear weapon was exploded, and Stalin's death. That event evidently released within the military bureaucracy, as elsewhere within the Soviet structure, ardent debate in which Stalin's pronouncements were no longer taken to be sacrosanct. And the debate was accompanied, if not in fact initiated in its most serious phase, by the successful explosion of a Soviet fusion weapon in August 1953.

Fusion weapons suddenly opened up new possibilities in the field of long-range missiles. Soviet experts, like those in the United States, had been working since 1945 with German technicians and their V-2 rocket. The V-2 had proved capable of hitting the London area regularly with a one-ton warhead from a range of 150–200 miles. The V-2 had been considerably refined in both countries in the period 1945–1952. The Soviet research and development effort was probably somewhat more substantial over these years, among other reasons because the intermediate ballistic missile—the first major stage beyond the V-2—was immensely significant for Soviet strategy since it could strike at American bases around the periphery of the Communist bloc. It is clear that down to 1953 Moscow also pursued at the research and development

16

level a major effort to create the long-range aircraft required for a modernized Soviet strategic air command.

In short, during the first eight postwar years, Soviet military authorities left open the possibility of developing delivery capabilities for weapons of mass destruction in the field of both long-range aircraft and ballistic missiles. But, until the fusion bomb was created, the long-range ballistic missile appeared as a relatively limited instrument of war. This was so primarily because the aiming error of rockets was so great and the destructive range of fission weapons so limited that damage to chosen targets was problematical. Thus the vastly enlarged area of destruction of the H-bomb, once it could be reduced in size to fit the nose cone of a rocket, elevated the military status of missiles. In the course of 1953 the long-range rocket for the first time became a weapon of self-evident and urgent operational interest.

During 1953 the Soviet authorities made a fundamental decision to proceed at full tilt with the development of intermediate- and long-range ballistic missiles. At the same time, the pace of development of the Soviet strategic air command was reduced. A Ministry of Defense Production charged with the production of missiles was set up in 1953; a special Committee on Space Travel, at the highest scientific level, was set up in 1954; and the ablest minds in the four most relevant fields of basic science evidently turned with increased operational emphasis to the missile problem—fluid dynamics and heat transfer, fuel chemistry and combustion, structures and materials, electronics and communication theory. In the course of 1954 the field of missiles technology invaded the Soviet engineering curriculum on a large scale.

This strategic decision undoubtedly appealed to Russian minds for several reasons. In the first place, although the Soviet Union had developed long-range aircraft and a long-range bombing force, it had not developed a strategic air command on anything like the scale of the American forces.

Moreover, the Second World War had not given the Russian air force experience in long-range mass flying, targeting, and navigation. Further, the American base structure and the air defense system rapidly building in North America during 1953 seemed to forecast a more or less permanent Soviet disadvantage. The Soviets may thus have felt that in relying for nuclear weapons delivery on a strategic air command they would be moving in behind a more experienced force and would be bound to remain somewhat inferior in this area. They may have felt in relation to the American Strategic Air Command somewhat as the Germans felt in relation to the British navy in the first half of the twentieth century.

On the other hand, there was no reason to believe that the Soviets were in any way behind the United States in missiles: Russia had a distinguished history of scientific contributions to rocketry reaching back to czarist times and had used short-range rockets extensively in the Second World War; the fundamental talents in the relevant fields of basic science and engineering were evidently available; and the missile business was in some of its dimensions an extension of artillery, in which Russia had traditionally excelled. Moreover, the whole enterprise appeared to provide a way of bypassing an enemy's main strength.

The 1953 decision to proceed at highest priority with missile development did not, however, settle post-Stalin military policy. The question arose: to what extent should the Soviet Union come to rely on the offensive and retaliatory power of ballistic missiles as opposed to modernized ground and naval forces? It is evident that in the course of 1954 the Soviet Union went through a major policy struggle in which the military fought against what they regarded as an excessive commitment of Malenkov to rely in the future on the ability to deliver nuclear weapons with ballistic missiles. Khrushchev openly argued against Malenkov on the balance of light versus heavy industry, in favor of the latter. And this abstract debate concealed an argument on the scale of the military budget and, especially, on the scale of allocations to more conventional military arms. Khrushchev's position on this matter may have gained him significant support from the military as he moved to dominance in the collective leadership.

In 1955, then, Soviet military policy consisted in a balanced program designed to produce as soon as possible intermediate- and long-range ballistic missiles; to modernize substantial if somewhat reduced infantry, artillery, and tactical air forces for atomic ground combat; to modernize the Soviet navy, at the expense of older vessels, notably to increase submarine missile delivery capabilities and to extend and refine air defense. This program was pursued for the rest of the decade, drawing off something like 20 percent of the Soviet gross national product.

But all this took time, and in nuclear delivery capabilities and in certain other fields the Soviet Union lagged considerably behind the United States. In the interval between the Soviet decision to give first priority to producing a missile delivery system and the time that operational tests were successfully completed—that is, from the end of 1953 to some time in 1956—Moscow pursued a policy designed to minimize the possibility of major war. The missiles were not in place, the Soviet bomber force was under limited development at best, and American delivery capabilities remained very substantial. From the Soviet perspective this was a time for relative tranquillity on the world scene. Thus, the Indochina clash was settled on reasonable terms, and the Austrian treaty was at last signed on May 5, 1955.

On May 10 the Soviet delegation at a United Nations meeting in London proposed a phased disarmament scheme which contained a provision which would provide for an international control authority manning "control posts at large ports, at railway junctions, on main motor highways and in aerodromes. The function of these posts shall be to ensure that no dangerous concentration of military land forces or of air or naval forces takes place." The full text of the Soviet inspection proposals and the initial reply of the U.S. delegate are given in Appendix C. The inspection feature represented something of a departure in Soviet policy and clearly required further exploration, although fixed inspection posts had been used in Korea and Indochina and proved a weak reed. It was in the relatively hopeful setting of the Austrian settlement and the Soviet inspection proposals that a summit conference was finally agreed among the four powers.

From the Soviet point of view, the mood of relaxed tension they wished to generate at the Geneva conference of 1955 had two major purposes. The first was to encourage complacency in the West and, in particular, to allay anxiety concerning the Soviet maneuvers in Asia, the Middle East, and Africa, which were beginning to accelerate at just this time. The second purpose was to induce the West to diminish the attention and outlays devoted to the arms race at a stage when the Soviets were pressing hard and hopefully to close the gap in weapons of mass destruction and to modernize their ground forces as well. The published Soviet military budget of 1955 was increased from 18 to 19 percent of Soviet GNP; American military outlays for goods and services in 1955 were reduced from 11.2 to 9.6 percent of GNP.

A third element appears to have played a part in the Soviet desire for a summit conference in 1955. As leaders of their nation and, indeed, as human beings, the new Soviet rulers wished to come out onto the world stage, to demonstrate they could comport themselves appropriately, with dignity, and to be accepted as world statesmen.

This desire was, no doubt, heightened by memories of Stalin's international stature during the Second World War and of his view that his successors would be unable to deal successfully with "the imperialists." These strands clearly emerge in Khrushchev's memoirs in passages of considerable credibility:

> Right up until his death Stalin used to tell us, "You'll see, when I'm gone the imperialistic powers will wring your

necks like chickens." We never tried to reassure him that we would be able to manage. . . .

After Stalin died it was an interesting challenge for us to try to deal with the foreign powers by ourselves. In 1955 we went abroad a number of times to meet with the representatives of the bourgeois states and to feel them out on various issues. Our trip to Geneva that year gave the bourgeois heads of state a chance to look us over. The Geneva meeting was a crucial test for us: Would we be able to represent our country competently? Would we approach the meeting soberly, without unrealistic hopes, and would we be able to keep the other side from intimidating us?[9]

And, again, Khrushchev recalled his reflections on the eve of his 1959 trip to the United States:

It's not that I was frightened, but I'll admit that I was worried. I felt as though I were about to undergo an important test.

We'd already passed the test in India, in Indonesia, and in England. [It was at Geneva that Khrushchev arranged with Eden to be invited to Britain.] But this was different—this was America. Not that we considered American culture to be on a higher plane than English culture, but American power was of decisive significance. Therefore our task would be both to represent our country with dignity, yet treat our negotiating partner with respect. You shouldn't forget that all during Stalin's life, right up to the day he died, he kept telling us we'd never be able to stand up to the forces of imperialism, that the first time we came into contact with the outside world our enemies would smash us to pieces; we would get confused and be unable to defend our land. In his words, we would become "agents" of some kind.[10]

These symbolic and human objectives were, of course, framed by serious and more conventional considerations. Among them, as noted earlier, was the fact that in the mid 1950s Soviet policy toward Asia, the Middle East, and Africa was shifting onto a new long-term basis. The switch occurred between the time that truce negotiations began in June 1951 and July 1953, when the Korean War was brought to a close. The essence of the new policy lay in the perception that the aspirations of the peoples and governments of Asia, the Middle East, and Africa could be turned to the purposes of Soviet power without the direct application of Soviet military force. Soviet policy included, starting in 1953, an effort to expand trade between the developing regions and the COMECON countries, and in 1954 a program of loans and technical assistance was launched. The operations were undertaken selectively, evidently reflecting Soviet strategic priorities or targets of opportunity. Much the most corrosive dimension of the new policy, from a Western perspective, was the arms deals. It was on June 9, 1955—just before the Geneva summit—that the U.S. ambassador in Cairo informed Washington that "tentative agreements" had been reached on the Soviet sale of arms to Egypt. The deal, formalized in September, set in motion a long chain of explosive events reaching down to the present day. More generally, the summit conference, with its acknowledgment by the West of Soviet status as a world power, was seen in Moscow as an event strengthening its activities in the developing regions.

Soviet policy toward Western Europe in the wake of Stalin's death was, thus, to encourage European hopes about Soviet pacific intentions while the foundations of Western European strength and influence and the foundations of the North Atlantic Alliance were gradually eroded by the expansion of Soviet military strength and the disruptions induced or heightened in Asia, the Middle East, and Africa. Whereas Europe was the direct and primary focus of Stalin's offensive, Europe was a target at one remove of the Soviet policy that emerged in 1953.

Immediately after Stalin's death Moscow launched a whole series of pacific gestures, some of which were designed to have a special impact on Western European thought. In a speech of March 16, 1953, before the Supreme Soviet, Malenkov made peace central to the posture of the new regime;

and starting at the end of March the Chinese Communists, backed by Molotov, accepted the United Nations offer to exchange sick and wounded prisoners. Moscow initiated discussions with Britain on air safety along the approaches to Berlin; a visit of American newspaper editors to the Soviet Union was organized; Soviet delegates put on a particularly businesslike performance at the East-West trade meetings of the United Nations Economic Commission for Europe in Geneva. A new willingness to expand contacts between Soviet and Western bureaucrats and intellectuals was indicated; and, above all, there was a massive demonstration of professional good-fellowship by Soviet diplomats at a variety of points where they were in contact with the external world.

All this stirred a powerful desire in Western Europe to enter promptly into negotiation with the Soviet Union on the abiding issues of Germany and the control of armaments, and in the summer of 1953 this desire was strongly enhanced by the explosion of the first Soviet fusion weapon.

For the first time since 1949 the four foreign ministers were finally brought together in Berlin at the end of January 1954. The three Western ministers, fearful of some new Soviet flexibility, found Molotov's position on Germany absolutely unchanged. There was every indication that Moscow was prepared to sit tight on the line of the Elbe. The one substantial result of the conference was to force a commitment from the West to meet in April, along with Communist China, on the issue of Indochina. And then, in May 1955, Moscow made the most impressive gesture of all for Europeans by signing the Austrian treaty and launched its intriguing proposal for mutual inspection of disarmament agreements via fixed posts. The pressure of public opinion in Western Europe for a serious negotiating effort with Moscow mounted to a point, for example, where the British Conservatives felt it imperative to hold a summit meeting before they next faced their electorate (see Appendix H, p. 162).

As for the United States, the factors that led Eisenhower

and Dulles to acquiesce in a summit meeting are tolerably clear: the problem of German rearmament had been successfully resolved, in the wake of the failure of the European Defense Community, by the emergence of the Western European Union; opinion in France was strongly for such a meeting and, after assuming the role of prime minister in April 1955, Eden reversed his earlier stance and joined Churchill in advocacy; the completion in May of the Austrian State Treaty provided Eisenhower something of "the actual deeds giving some indication of a Communist readiness to negotiate constructively . . ."; and, at home, support for such a gathering was on the rise, led by Walter George, chairman of the Senate Foreign Relations Committee.[11] Eisenhower concludes: "Because of the Soviet's action, and not wishing to appear senselessly stubborn in my attitude toward a Summit meeting—so hopefully desired by so many—I instructed Secretary Dulles to let it be known through diplomatic channels, that if other powers were genuinely interested in such a meeting we were ready to listen to their reasoning."[12] Dulles took this instruction with him to Paris on May 6, where, at a NATO meeting, agreement was reached with the British, French, and Germans to invite the Soviet Union to a summit meeting. The invitation was dispatched to Moscow on May 10 and discussed with Molotov a few days later in Vienna on the occasion of the signing of the Austrian State Treaty. By June 13 formal agreement was reached, although it had been foreshadowed for some time. A week later the foreign ministers met in San Francisco on the occasion of the tenth anniversary of the signing of the United Nations Charter and went some distance in settling the procedures to be followed. Dulles' concept, as described by Eisenhower, was this: "He proposed a five-day meeting in Geneva, during which the heads of government would attempt only to define the crucial world problems and then issue a directive to the Foreign Ministers to work out the details and conduct negotiations."[13]

The notion of putting the president of the United States on the world stage for five days "only to define" the world's problems seemed neither sensible nor viable to one member of Eisenhower's staff, Nelson Rockefeller. Indeed, he had already proceeded, through correct bureaucratic channels, to set things in motion in another direction by a somewhat unorthodox bureaucratic device. The two chapters that follow chronicle the consequences of this difference in views about what the president of the United States should do at Geneva.

3. The Quantico Panel, June 5-10, 1955

Shortly after it was decided that a summit meeting was likely, Nelson Rockefeller and his staff organized a group of eleven men to take stock of where the United States stood in the world and to recommend courses of action for the president at the summit. All were from outside the mainstream of the bureaucracies but professionally knowledgeable in one or another aspect of national security affairs. Rockefeller had succeeded C. D. Jackson as a presidential aide in December 1954. His status was somewhat more formal than his predecessor's. Rockefeller was not only a member of the Operations Coordinating Board, chaired by the undersecretary of state, Herbert Hoover, Jr., but was also chairman of a special subcommittee designed "to exploit Sino-Soviet vulnerabilities." It was from this base that he launched, with Eisenhower's knowledge and agreement, the enterprise with which this chapter is concerned.

Rockefeller also operated in a somewhat different way than had Jackson. He recruited a small staff, mainly within the government, headed by an army brigadier general of wide background, Theodore W. Parker. On the staff, and of considerable influence, was William R. Kintner, an army colonel also with broad experience and interests. He played a major role in suggesting the Quantico exercise, recruiting its personnel, and was present throughout. Like Jackson, Rockefeller sought outside advice; but he did so in a more organized manner. As we shall see in Chapter 4, his working style as well as the policies he came to advocate were to create some serious problems in the government.

Those participating in the Quantico venture were Frederick Dunn, director, Center of International Studies, Princeton University; C. D. Jackson, Time-Life; Ellis A. Johnson, director, Operations Research Office; Paul Linebarger, School of Advanced International Studies, Johns Hopkins University; Max Millikan, Center for International Studies, MIT; Philip Mosely, director, Russian Institute, Columbia University; George Pettee, deputy director, Operations Research Office; Stefan Possony, air intelligence specialist, Department of the Air Force; W. W. Rostow, Center for International Studies, MIT; Hans Speier, RAND Corporation; and Charles A. H. Thomson, the Brookings Institution. I was asked by Rockefeller to chair the meetings.

The only contemporary account of what actually went on at Quantico, of which I am aware, is that of C. D. Jackson. He had the wit to set down, in August 1955, after checking with participants, the whole sequence of events from Quantico to Geneva (see Appendix D). A contemporary recording of the post-Quantico sequence was also done by General Parker (dated August 3, 1955). Although he was there for a number of the sessions, Parker does not deal with the dynamics of the Quantico meeting. His record includes, however, a useful collection of relevant documents (see Appendix E).

Jackson was present at the opening meeting on Sunday night, June 5. He returned to New York to reappear on June 8–9. A presentation of our conclusions was made to a considerable group of Washington officials on the latter evening, including Allen Dulles, Stassen, and, perhaps most important for later events, Andrew Goodpaster, Eisenhower's almost invisible but influential aide. Except for Walworth Barbour's appearance at the initial Sunday night session, no major State Department official attended, for reasons which will emerge and which Jackson's account in Appendix D makes clear.

So far as my memory serves, Jackson's portrait of the dishevelment on Sunday night and the relative unity and order three days later is quite accurate. What happened, as nearly as I can recall, was this.

After a typically discursive initial meeting on Sunday night, we spent Monday going around the table providing each member of the group an opportunity to state what he thought the report ought to contain. As one would expect, the participants brought to the occasion their accumulated intellectual capital, which proved both rich and diverse. Isolated as we were on a Marine Corps base, relatively few in number as such committees go, there was plenty of time; and, besides, it rained a good deal during the week. I believe we got through the individual statements on Monday. On Tuesday we began to weave them into the pattern of a report. Before dinner on Tuesday some clear notions had emerged, and I proposed the following.

1. The report should contain a terse summary and recommendations containing the major strategic conclusions at which we had arrived and, related to them, our proposals for the summit.

2. A relatively brief but longer text elaborating the bases for the strategy and summit proposals.

3. Appendixes underpinning major elements in the argument on which there was wide, if not universal, agreement.

4. Individual supporting papers in which each participant, in his own name, could file with the report a statement of his views on any subject he judged to be germane.

I volunteered to produce overnight a draft of the basic strategy and recommendations for the summit on which my colleagues could work the next day while I caught up on sleep. This procedure was possible because three basic ideas crystallized in the course of the Monday and Tuesday sessions.

First, a strategic conclusion. This was brought into sharp focus, in substantial part, due to the exposition of Ellis Johnson, director of the Operations Research Office, a unit working with the army in something like the way RAND worked with the air force. Johnson presented the results of a detailed study of relative U.S.-U.S.S.R. technical military capabilities (see Appendix F). It exhibited the leads and lags as of the mid 1940s and mid 1950s for types of aircraft, ordnance tanks, electronics, and the size of the pool of scientific and technical personnel. In general, it showed a marked narrowing of the Soviet lags, where they existed, and the remarkable postwar buildup of highly trained Soviet scientists and engineers. It was the sort of analysis that was to become quite familiar later in the 1950s, notably in the wake of the launching of the first Sputnik in October 1957. Along with a good deal of other evidence laid on the table, including detailed analyses of the NATO-Warsaw Pact and the nuclear balance of forces, Johnson's exposition impressed us with the notion that the U.S. enjoyed, as of mid 1955, a net military advantage that was narrowing and would prove transient if current trends continued and that the summit should be used as a test of the seriousness of Soviet peaceful intentions.

Second, we hit on a method to make such a test and to do so in ways which both met the American interest in presenting itself as a power seriously interested in peace and gave the president scope for considerable personal initiative. The method was to have the president initiate during the week in Geneva a spectrum of proposals ranging from hard to soft, that is, proposals which the Soviet Union would accept only if its intent was substantially to liquidate the Cold War down to proposals which might well be accepted if Soviet interests in a pacific posture were merely transient and tactical.

At the hard end of the spectrum we suggested proposals for the unification of Germany and for graduated disarmament. It was in the latter context that the concept of mutual aerial inspections arose, in a manner outlined below. The general concept behind it was that serious arms control agreements could not occur unless each side knew with some confidence the force structure of the other. Inspection had, therefore, to be tested before arms control agreements were finally concluded.

The other suggested proposals included the offer by the president of agreements to expand East-West trade, increase the freedom of persons to travel anywhere in the world for peaceful purposes, provide for free and unhampered international communication of information and ideas, pool information and facilities for the exploration of peaceful uses of atomic energy, and generate a worldwide fund for the economic development of underdeveloped areas.

So far as the Quantico Panel was concerned, mutual aerial inspection was proposed on Tuesday afternoon by Max Millikan as an element in our report. He later told Jackson (see Appendix D) that he heard the idea discussed at an arms control session in Cambridge. It was quickly seized upon and put into our spectrum of proposals. But one member of the group, Hans Speier of RAND, was disturbed. He took Possony and me aside and said that the proposal was dangerous and he would have to inform air intelligence immediately that we were thinking of putting forward the idea. (Possony was a civilian working for air intelligence and also closely associated with Rockefeller's staff.) Neither Possony nor I thought the idea dangerous, even if, as Speier guardedly implied, the United States might be generating plans for unilateral aerial photography of the U.S.S.R. I suggested that we append the following footnote at several points in the report when the proposal was mentioned: "Aside from our general assumption that before implementation all these suggestions will be considered carefully by the Departments, it is recommended that this proposal be examined with particular scepticism by the Department of Defense."

Here is the form in which mutual aerial inspection was proposed in the Quantico Panel report:

> 1. An agreement for mutual inspection of military installations, weapons, and armaments. Until experience has been

developed on the feasibility of such inspection, this agreement would make no provision for arms limitation. Its purpose would be to provide knowledge and evidence on the basis of which a control plan could be devised.

2. A convention insuring the right of aircraft of any nationality to fly freely over the territory of any country for peaceful purposes. The possibility of abuse of this right could be prevented by the establishment of safely located control points for the international inspection and registration of aircraft for flights across international boundaries. The convention would be so drawn as not to interfere in any way with any nation's right to control for economic reasons commercial activities of foreign aircraft.

The third proposition on which we came to agreement followed directly from the assessment that the Soviet Union was narrowing the gap between its own and U.S. capabilities and from the notion of a spectrum of proposals to test the Soviet willingness to move forward on a peaceful basis. It was that, should the Geneva conference reveal Soviet unwillingness to deal seriously with the critical issues of arms control and Germany, as we expected it would, U.S. policy would have to face up to an enlarged military budget and a more energetic policy in other dimensions. This is how I concluded a personal letter to Rockefeller reflecting on the panel's report (the full text is given in Appendix G):

> Set this letter aside now. Perhaps Geneva will reveal that my timing is off and we can proceed directly and seriously to peace. But read it again if what we see is merely a clever playing for time, an effort to disrupt the unity and to diminish the effort of the West with gestures and blandishments. For then it will be the time to say to the American people that at the highest level we found no serious intent to end the arms race; and that the protection of our society requires a higher level of effort or sacrifice.

With these three propositions agreed, it was not difficult to have a draft of the final report in the hands of my colleagues by breakfast on Wednesday. On Wednesday morning the members of the panel refined the draft; in the afternoon, when I rejoined the group, we decided on and assigned drafting responsibilities for four major appendixes to be part of the report itself:

Appendix A—*Estimate of the Situation*
Appendix B—*Proposals to Test Soviet Willingness to Make Concessions and to Improve the U.S. Position* [including mutual aerial inspection]
Appendix C—*The German Question*
    1.—Preliminary Diplomatic Action in Preparation for the Summit Conference
    2.—U.S. Guidelines for a German Settlement
    3.—German Elections
    4.—Possible Proposals for German Unity
Appendix D—*A Proposal for Graduated Disarmament*

Others went to work on their supporting papers.[14] By Wednesday evening, as Jackson's account suggests, we were rolling along in pretty good shape.

On Thursday, the final substantive day of the conference, we worked on the drafts and prepared for the presentation of our results to Rockefeller and those who had accepted his invitation to attend the briefing. As noted earlier, Stassen, Allen Dulles, and Goodpaster were present. The State Department was, as best I can recall, not represented. A good deal of time was spent on the proposal for mutual aerial inspection, which was, clearly, something of a surprise. Stassen, the senior arms control negotiator, appeared to have some difficulty understanding the rationale for the concept; but there was a general sense among our guests that, rather to their surprise, a reasonably coherent and substantive report had emerged. As we shall see, expectations had not been high in some quarters.

On Friday, July 10, the report, its appendixes, annexes, and a formal letter of transmittal to Rockefeller were duly completed, and the package went forward into the bureaucracy.

The letter of transmittal included this passage:

> We have no expectation that we have produced either a magic formula for positive U.S. action or a substitute for the staff considerations currently under way in the responsible Government Departments. We offer these recommendations and the papers that underlie them as a supplement to those considerations. It is our hope that responsible officials will find our efforts constructive and that use can be made of the many concrete suggestions included in the Panel results.

4. From Quantico to Geneva: June 10 to July 21, 1955

The bureaucratic sequence from Quantico to Geneva, so far as the Open Skies proposal is concerned, is well set out in Parker's chronology prefacing his assembly of documents bearing on the matter (see Appendix E):

5–10 June	Quantico Panel. One of the most significant recommendations of their report was the one proposing mutual inspection, including overflight.
10–30 June	Efforts were made to generate interest in Quantico Report, particularly the mutual inspection proposal. No results. Wide distribution was made of the Report, including copies to the President, State Department, Defense Department, and Mr. Stassen.
30 June	Mr. Stassen reported to the NSC on the results of his disarmament study. No conclusion. The President directed that an inspection system be carefully studied. [Rockefeller was not present.]
6 July	Nelson Rockefeller handcarried to the President a memorandum strongly recommending approval of the mutual inspection proposal (as described in the Quantico Report) and use of it at the Big Four conference. The President called the Secretary of State on the telephone and expressed his

	interest. The Secretary said they were studying it.
11–13 July	In spite of opposition, Nelson Rockefeller arranged for himself and small staff to proceed to Paris for the period of Big Four conference (subject to call to Geneva). In preparation for the Conference, Nelson Rockefeller prepared a document, "Psychological Strategy at Geneva," copies of which were furnished the President, the Secretary of State, Mr. Dillon Anderson, and Colonel Goodpaster. The issue of disarmament was covered in this document, utilizing the mutual inspection proposal as the U.S. position. The strategy of handling the proposal was outlined, and a draft statement for use of the President drafted.
18 July	The mutual inspection proposal was discussed by Nelson Rockefeller in Paris in conference with Mr. Stassen, Mr. Anderson, Mr. Gray and Adm Radford. Adm Radford showed keen interest. The others showed interest, but with reservations.
19 July A.M.	Another meeting was held with Mr. Anderson, Mr. Stassen and Adm Radford. Mr. Anderson and Adm Radford, in a message of comments on the conference opening statements, addressed to the Secretary of State at Geneva, included a paragraph regarding the importance of the inspection issue. In the discussion following, Mr. Stassen concurred in a statement Nelson Rockefeller had drafted for the President on the subject, and suggested minor changes in the draft.
19 July	As revised, this statement was sent by Nelson Rockefeller to Colonel Goodpaster at 1315 hours. Later in the day Nelson Rockefeller and Mr. Stassen were directed to proceed to Geneva on 20 July.

20 July A.M.	The President discussed the mutual inspection proposal with Nelson Rockefeller and Mr. Stassen. He said that he had discussed the proposal at breakfast with Prime Minister Eden who was enthusiastic. The President stated that he wanted Adm Radford to come to Geneva right away. He also said that Eden wanted Gen. Brownjohn to discuss the proposal with Gen. Gruenther.
20 July P.M.	Another meeting was held on the proposal. Present were the President, Nelson Rockefeller, Dulles, Merchant, Stassen, Anderson, Radford and Gruenther, latter three having arrived from Paris. A statement prepared by Stassen on Dulles' direction was used as basis of discussion. Dulles strongly supported proposal at this meeting.
21 July A.M.	Further conferences were held and the draft statement was polished. The tactics of presentation were planned by the President.
21 July P.M.	The President made the mutual inspection proposal in plenary session of the conference, using the prepared statement plus additional remarks along lines suggested by Nelson Rockefeller.

What the chronology does not capture is the curious bureaucratic and personal struggle which characterizes the story down to Geneva and beyond. Its central figure is Nelson Rockefeller and the opposition he generated within the Eisenhower administration in the course of 1955. There was also, as we shall see, a deep underlying anxiety on the part of John Foster Dulles about the summit meeting and what might transpire at Geneva. These had the effect of his seeking to narrow the president's role. Taken together, these concerns complicated the translation of the Quantico concept into a presidential proposal.

Dulles had been uneasy about the Quantico venture from the beginning. The beginning was in May, when agreement on a summit meeting was crystallizing in the wake of the conclusion of the Austrian State Treaty and Soviet disarmament proposals of May 10, which included the possibility of mutual inspection from fixed posts on the ground. The OCB (Operations Coordinating Board), a committee at the undersecretary level in which Rockefeller participated, had approved the creation of the Quantico Panel, as had Eisenhower. The terms of reference of the panel, as understood by the president, were, however, somewhat vague. They related to the summit, but the task of the panel was defined somewhere in the ambiguous area of "psychological warfare." Rockefeller's memory of the Quantico framework, in an oral history interview, is fairly consistent with this ambiguity, although clearly the Geneva conference and what the president might do there were on his mind; and this dimension of our task was clearly transmitted to the members of the Quantico Panel:

> So Ted [Parker] working with this colonel [Kintner] picked these people who were academicians and we went to Quantico for a series of sessions. Their assignment was: How do you view the world scene and world problems and what posture should the United States take? What can the President's position be?[15]

The matter came to a head on May 25. The president's diary (kept from Eisenhower's dictation by his personal secretary, Mrs. Ann Whitman) includes this passage: "President said that Dulles at lunch had said that Nelson was calling a conference to determine policy to be followed at Summit Conference. President had defended Nelson saying that he had no such intention."[16] Eisenhower nevertheless called in Rockefeller, received assurances on Quantico, and called Dulles at 2:46 P.M. Notes on the conversation, made by Dulles' secretary, Phyllis Bernau, follow:

TELEPHONE CALL FROM THE PRESIDENT

The Pres. got Nelson in and re Quantico—it has nothing to do with the 4-Power Mtg. He has appointed himself a consultative body to study foreign reactions to things— heads of universities are on it. It advises on psychological warfare. (This sounds vague, but evidently they discussed it at lunch.)[17]

The vagueness noted by Dulles' secretary was, one can suspect, purposeful on the part of the president. On the one hand, he was not about to let the Quantico Panel or Rockefeller "determine policy," as Dulles had defined his concern at lunch; nor was he about to let Rockefeller supplant Dulles in his position of primary adviser in foreign affairs. On the other hand, he was looking for ideas and had found that the rubric of "psychological warfare" within which C. D. Jackson and Rockefeller worked in 1953–1955 could embrace the generation of some valuable substantive proposals, for example, the post-Stalin peace speech of April 16, 1953, and the Atoms for Peace proposal made at the United Nations on December 8, 1953. In short, Eisenhower was seeking to keep both men at work for him and reasonably happy. It proved rather difficult.

Rockefeller's problems with Dulles and Dulles' problems with Rockefeller were deeper than the Quantico venture. By May 25, in fact, Rockefeller indicated to the president, in response to a query from him, that in the light of his difficulties with the State Department he would consider taking the post of deputy secretary of defense. Robert Anderson had filled the job since May 1954 and indicated he wished to resign. Eisenhower had urged him to remain at his post. Here is the relevant note of May 25, 1955, from the Whitman diary:

> Later in the afternoon President asked Nelson if he had decided what to do about the job as Deputy Director of De-

fense. Nelson implied that it was so difficult to work with State that he might favorably consider, in case President did not urge Bob Anderson to reconsider [leaving].

President didn't see how he could; later he said to acw [Mrs. Whitman] that he would write to some of his Texas friends if he knew how to put it on paper. May write, may not.[18]

In fact, Anderson stayed on until August 1955, and Rockefeller carried on as special assistant down to the end of the year.

From Dulles' point of view, Rockefeller represented an acute case of a general problem which Sherman Adams describes well in his memoir. After evoking Dulles' vivid memory of how his uncle, Secretary of State Robert Lansing, and Cordell Hull had been substantially bypassed by Wilson and Franklin Roosevelt, Adams goes on:

> In order to help him keep in the closest touch with the economic and military problems of foreign policy, Eisenhower appointed special assistants in those areas to work directly under the White House and side by side with the State Department. It was a delicate experiment. While they represented the President, these assistants assumed theoretically none of the prerogatives of Foster Dulles or any other Cabinet Secretary. They were expediters and coordinators, but they were also men capable of creating new approaches to the solution of problems which divided the world. From time to time, Dulles found in his diplomatic domain such presidential assistants as Harold Stassen in mutual security, foreign operations and disarmament, Lewis Strauss in atomic energy affairs, C. D. Jackson in cold war psychology planning, Clarence Randall and Joseph Dodge in foreign economic policy and Walter George and James Richards as special consultants in foreign affairs. The President made none of these appointments without Dulles' full approval. Still, Dulles watched these specialists intently and, at the first sign of what he suspected to be a possible threat to the tight and straight line-of-command between himself and the President, he straightened out the difficulty quickly. If he thought

he couldn't straighten it out himself, he did not hesitate to take it to me and finally to Eisenhower. In every instance where Dulles decided the situation was intolerable, he insisted on a change, and the President without exception went along with his wishes. Jackson's job as a foreign policy idea man infringed delicately on Dulles' official bailiwick, but Jackson knew how to handle the Secretary and always managed to get along with him cordially. Nelson Rockefeller, who succeeded Jackson, had no such success. Nor did Stassen, whose diplomatic missions drove Dulles to such distraction that Stassen's work for the President in foreign affairs was finally brought to an end. Rockefeller's working methods, in contrast to those of Jackson, annoyed Dulles. Jackson had worked alone, with little or no staff. He formed his own ideas and put them to work in close collaboration with the Secretary. When Rockefeller, on the other hand, went to work on a dramatic peace plan that could be presented by Eisenhower at the 1955 summit conference at Geneva, he organized a large group of technical experts, researchers, and idea men and moved them into seclusion at the Marine Base at Quantico, Virginia, away from Dulles and the State Department. The air of secrecy around the Rockefeller operation and the number of people involved in it made Dulles apprehensive. "He seems to be building up a big staff," Dulles said to me suspiciously one day. "He's got them down at Quantico, and nobody knows what they're doing."

Eventually the Quantico Panel, as the Rockefeller study group was called, came up with the open-skies inspection plan, which Eisenhower believed workable, not simply as a new weapon in the cold war, but as a possible breakthrough in the disarmament stalemate. Although Dulles would have been skeptical of any proposal coming from the Rockefeller operation, the lukewarm attitude that he took toward the open-skies plan was based mainly on his doubt that anything would come of it.[19]

It was natural for Rockefeller to operate with a staff as he had done in the other public posts he had held, and it was also his style to assemble expert groups to study specific problems that interested him. Both at the time and in retrospect, Dulles' reaction to the assembly at Quantico of a rather harmless group of well-meaning characters seemed excessive, as was his reaction to Rockefeller's rather modest personal staff. But his concern was no doubt heightened by two other aspects of Rockefeller's performance. When Rockefeller decided an idea was sound and deserved advocacy, he plunged into the task of salesmanship with verve. He did, indeed, usually make sure that Dulles was informed; but he was never content to stop there. Following is a somewhat anguished memorandum of a conversation between Sherman Adams and Dulles arising from a Rockefeller proposal for a presidential speech containing ideas generated by Theodore Repplier, then working with the Advertising Council. Dulles had evidently received the memorandum but was disturbed that it had gone to the president before it had been "staffed more properly."

August 5, 1955
6:08 P.M.

TELEPHONE CALL FROM GOVERNOR ADAMS

A. [Adams] asked if the President has spoken to the Sec about the Rockefeller memorandum. The Sec said all he (the Sec) had said was he was having a lot of trouble and he wanted the Pres to know what a headache it was for him. This had opened a broader discussion than had been anticipated. The Sec said he had discussed the matter with Adams. A. said Nelson had not followed his discussion with him. The Sec said he had repeated to the Pres his concept of the job Rockefeller should do, picking out nuggets from personal visits and letters. He should not build up a big staff; this was duplicating other Departments' work. A. said the memo had to do with the Repplier idea re a speech and changing some policies, it would take a tremendous amount of thought and work. A. said he thought it was understood R. would talk to the Sec, but instead he writes you a memo and the President a longer memo which should not be done. R. had quoted A.

that he thought well of it, which he did but would not think of bothering the Pres with it now. The Sec said he did not know about Repplier but he thought the Pres had mentioned it and said it should not have come in until staffed more properly. A. said of course it should not have, and this is indicative of the fact that we may have made progress but it is hardly perceptible. A. said he does not feel R. can operate as Jackson did, and it raises the whole question of whether he should continue to serve in this capacity. A. said we could not have him running to the other agencies saying the Pres or A. likes this or that.[20]

Earlier on the same day, Dulles had raised formally with the president Rockefeller's status and method:

August 5, 1955

Personal and Private
EYES ONLY

MEMORANDUM OF CONVERSATION
WITH THE PRESIDENT
12:30
Subject: Nelson Rockefeller

I raised with the President the situation re Nelson Rockefeller, stating that I simply wanted the President to know at this stage that we were having a very difficult time working with him and that, although I was trying to work the situation out, I was not at all sure that I would be successful in doing so. I then described to the President briefly my own thinking as to the proper role that someone in Rockefeller's position should play. I said that I felt that his primary function was to screen the many ideas, written and oral, that came into the White House in the field of foreign affairs and to see to it that the worthwhile ones were put into proper Government channels for further consideration and followed up. I said that I recognized that the regular departments were often so tied to daily routines that they did not have time or resourcefulness in dealing with new ideas. However, I said that if somebody like Nelson Rockefeller built up a staff of his own, as he appeared to have every intention of doing, he in turn became a bureaucrat and defeated the whole purpose of the exercise.

I then showed the President the copy of the memorandum Governor Adams had given me from Nelson Rockefeller to the President outlining his staff requirements. The President expressed some surprise at the size and complexity of the proposed staff and said that he had been unaware of all these arrangements.

S RLO'Connor:mfl:ma[21]

And on August 11 Adams and Dulles discussed further "the cross they were bearing":

> THURSDAY
> August 11, 1955
> 3:05 P.M.

TELEPHONE CALL FROM GOV. ADAMS

A. asked if the Sec. had a satisfactory talk with Rockefeller. The Sec. said he didn't know—we didn't have a decisive talk. He told of some of his plans and I am not awfully happy with it. I can live with it if it does not get any worse. A. said for them to watch it. The Sec. said he is trying to bring him in on things and make him feel part of things. He is making a terrible drain on time of myself and Hoover and now that we are trying to cultivate him, he absorbs a lot of time with his ideas. But it is better to have the ideas come to us than to the Pres. It is a cross to bear. We can get along for a while and see how it works out. The Sec. said he does not know how long he can afford the time. A. said if the Sec. thinks more therapy is needed, he better speak about it. A. would like to keep it out of the boss' hair. The Sec. said he didn't mention it today to the Pres. The Sec. said he can get along until next winter and see what happens. A. said if he thinks differently, to let him know.[22]

Rockefeller was clearly not a man who would, in Dulles' phrase, confine himself to "picking out nuggets from personal visits and letters"; but a more important element in the conflict was, essentially, a matter of personality. Rockefeller's style differed from C. D. Jackson's. Both were authentically warm and considerate men. Both were capable of taking strong positions and defending them before the president even against the views of the secretary of state. But, as Appendix H indicates, Jackson dealt with Dulles (and others) with elements of deference, compassion, supportiveness, and even flattery, all of which, I suspect, Rockefeller felt were inappropriate between strong men bearing serious responsibilities for public business. Rockefeller fought for his ideas with exuberance; and, in his own phrase, describing an incident dealt with later in this volume (see below, p. 49), he aptly remarked: "Being somewhat less than fully restrained in my approach to life. . . ."[23]

All this helps explain Dulles' reaction to the Quantico exercise. Here, for example, is a memorandum of a telephone conversation between Dulles and his brother Allen (AWD) on the day of the final Quantico briefing (June 9):

> . . . The Sec. asked if AWD is going to Nelson Rockefeller's show. Tonight. The Sec. wants to play it down. Doesn't think much of it. AWD wondered too. AWD did promise to go once and N. would be disappointed if he didn't. They agreed nothing would probably come of it. The Sec. said he [Rockefeller] went off on his own without any prior consultation. AWD will report.[24]

It also explains some of the odd situations that are embedded in Parker's chronology given at the opening of this chapter.

First, there was a rather sterile interval (June 10–30) when, Parker notes correctly, Rockefeller tried without much success to stir interest in the Quantico report. He circulated it widely and enlisted C. D. Jackson to write letters (on June 13) to Eisenhower and Dulles (see Appendix I). Jackson's letter to Dulles evokes rather vividly, in one passage, the inhospitable bureaucratic environment into which the Quantico report was inserted:

I have just returned from the very interesting and exhilarating Quantico meeting set up by Nelson Rockefeller, and I wanted to send you this note to express the hope that the document produced there will not get too automatic a brushoff in the tepees.

I can fully appreciate the instinctive irritation of a large number of intelligent, conscientious, seven-day-a-week, fifty-two-weeks-a-year professionals at what may appear to them to be a one-shot, off-the-top-of-the-head effort by some ad hoc enthusiasts.

I think the effort was considerably better than that, and merits your personal perusal—at least the opening "Report" section.

On June 30 Rockefeller returned to his office, having, presumably, been out of town and having thereby missed a rather important NSC meeting. As a memorandum from Parker noted (see Appendix E), the NSC session had been almost wholly devoted to a discussion of a U.S. plan for disarmament. The upshot was a directive to Stassen to come up with a "workable, satisfactory inspection system, if such exists." It was agreed that the work should not be hurried and that results would not, therefore, be available for the Geneva summit, less than three weeks away. Parker urged Rockefeller to recommend to the president, Dulles, and Stassen that the Quantico mutual inspection proposal be considered in addition to the Stassen plan. Round about noon on July 6, Rockefeller acted on Parker's advice, hand-carrying to Eisenhower a two-page memorandum, echoing in many respects the advice he had received a week earlier from his staff (see Appendix E).

Eisenhower reacted promptly, as he often did, by calling Dulles on the telephone. Dulles' files contain the following report of the conversation:

July 6, 1955
12:17 P.M.

The Pres. said he just heard of an idea that might open a tiny gate in the disarmament fence. We set up two groups to study and develop a plan for immediately starting inspection of each other's armament now to determine the utility of the systems before we proceed. The Sec. said that is his idea— he told Stassen that was the way to get started. The Soviets so offered in their May 10 plan and the Sec. said we should take them up on it. It is not the last word but it is a beginning and would get us out of the realm of just thinking about it. The Sec. said he wanted to get it into our NSC paper. The Pres. wished he could have used it this morning [when disarmament came up at a press conference]. Nelson was in talking to him about it. The Pres. said as long as the Sec. was thinking of it, he was satisfied.[25]

Rockefeller's 1977 memory of the July 6 intervention with the president is a bit more colorful:

I went to President Eisenhower with this idea because I thought it was very good. The thesis was that he was going to have to take the initiative and it had to be bold and it had to be something that immediately electrified everybody because it was so conceptually sound and universal in its application and its appeal. He immediately reacted in favor of it.

And he picked up the phone which was a habit he had and said what he had said on other occasions which got me into similar trouble. He called up Foster Dulles and said, "Nelson is here and he has got a tremendous idea." He then described the idea. I couldn't hear but the President said that Foster Dulles said that they had already studied this and discarded it as being of no interest and the President should not consider it.[26]

It should be recalled that what Dulles had in mind, as indicated by the memorandum of conversation in his files, was building on the Soviet May 10 proposal with its fixed inspection posts on the ground. On the basis of experience in

Asia, Eisenhower had concluded these would be ineffective. He saw much greater opportunity in mutual aerial inspection. I would guess that it was Rockefeller's memorandum of July 6 which firmly fixed in Eisenhower's mind that there was a disarmament proposal available for him to use at Geneva, although he did not, of course, firmly decide to go forward with it until July 20–21.

As the Geneva conference came closer there were three matters for Eisenhower to settle: the strategy to pursue, the content of his talk to the American people before leaving and his opening statement at the conference, and who should accompany him to Geneva. Dulles had strong and lucid views on all of them. He believed the president should offer no new initiatives but should confine himself to helping generate a spirit in which later detailed negotiations on such critical matters as Germany and disarmament might succeed; his preliminary talk to the American people should explicitly state that objective (see Appendix J). Dulles' suggestions of July 13 for Eisenhower's talk on the eve of his departure for Geneva included this passage:

> . . . What is the purpose? It is not primarily to find quick solutions—quickies don't work out in these matters. They prove to be disillusioning. They give a superficial interpretation, which leads to differences in the future. These complex problems can only be finally resolved by painstaking effort, thinking out of every detail—that is the stage that has to be right. But during these ten years that have ensued since the end of the Second World War, there have been many conferences that have tried to solve problems as merely technical things. They have all been just frustrations, struggles for power, propaganda battles—to pursue the problems that way is barren.
>
> The purpose of this trip primarily is to see and help others, to generate new spirit, satisfy their longings and aspirations, demanding a way that should be sound, sparing them and their children the devastations of another war.

Evidently, Dulles' image of the president's mission failed to answer a simple operational question: what should the president actually do in Geneva to generate a new spirit capable of suffusing subsequent technical negotiations with fresh vitality?

Given Dulles' limited view of the president's objective, only the secretary of state among the president's major advisers—not even Stassen the disarmament negotiator—was required to go to Geneva. Behind this impulse to narrow the president's role and his entourage lay not only a bureaucratic concern for the secretary of state's primacy but also deep inner fears, which he confided to C. D. Jackson at a private dinner on July 11 (see Appendix H).

After expressing some concern for the sturdiness of the British and French, Dulles, in Jackson's contemporary memorandum of conversation, went on as follows:

> "But what I am most worried about is the President. He and I have a relationship, both personal and operating, that has rarely existed between a Secretary of State and his President. As you know, I have nothing but admiration and respect for him, both as a person and as a man aware of foreign policy and conference pitfalls. Yet he is so inclined to be humanly generous, to accept a superficial tactical smile as evidence of inner warmth, that he might in a personal moment with the Russians accept a promise or a proposition at face value and upset the apple cart. Don't forget that informal buffet dinners will be the regular procedure every day, at which time I estimate the real work will be done, and it is at that time that I am particularly afraid that the Russians may get in their 'real work' with the President. . . .
>
> "The President likes things to be right, and pleasant, between people. He tires when an unpleasantness is dragged out indefinitely. . . ."

After rambling around on various details, Dulles said: "You know, I may have to be the Devil at Geneva, and I dread the prospect. . . .

"To my mind this is much more serious than the way we

have been discussing it. In fact, this is something that I have never breathed to a soul, or even intimated, and I suppose there is not anybody else I could actually say it to. My big problem is a personal problem. I am afraid that either something will go wrong in Geneva, some slip of the allies, some slip of the President's, which will put me in the position of having to go along with a kind of foreign policy for the U.S. which could be described as appeasement—no, appeasement is too strong a word, but you know what I mean—or, on the other hand, I may have to behave in such a way at Geneva that my usefulness as Secretary of State, both domestically and abroad, will come to an end."

Rockefeller contested Dulles' view of the appropriate role for Eisenhower on the grounds that it was simply impossible for the president of the United States to appear passively on the world stage for five days, while leaders of other governments proposed all manner of initiatives. Here is how Rockefeller in 1977 recalled a critical confrontation on the matter:

> So at that meeting he [Dulles] said, "Now, Mr. President, the way we are going to handle this is you will go to the conference and you will identify the problem areas and then you will suggest that these be given to the Ministers of Foreign Affairs to come up with solutions for these areas."
>
> Being somewhat less than fully restrained in my approach to life I said, "Mr. President, you can't do that. This is an impossible position. Number one, the Soviets and probably the British and the French will already have come up with ideas for solutions so that you are going to be caught flatfooted and nobody is going to take seriously that General Eisenhower, President Eisenhower, comes all the way to Geneva to a summit meeting and says I am going to identify the problems and give them to the Secretaries of Foreign Affairs to solve." I said, "That is an impossible position psychologically for the world. They are all looking to you again in this time of tension for leadership."
>
> HM [Hugh Morrow]: What did Foster Dulles' face look like when you said that?

NAR: I don't remember. But he said, "That is impossible, Mr. President. We have studied all these things and the way I have suggested is the way it should be." And the President said, "Nelson you have heard Foster. This is not acceptable and this is the way it is going to be."

So I came back twice more at what I thought were possible openings and the third time he [Eisenhower] really got mad, as he could do, and said, "God damnit [*sic*], I have told you we are not going to do that. Now stop talking about it. We are not going to follow this course of action. We are going to do what Foster recommends." I said, "Yes, sir."[27]

Although this interview was evidently conducted without notes some twenty-two years after the event, it conforms closely in substance to Rockefeller's contemporary account to me of what was going on in the days before the president's departure for Geneva.

But Eisenhower didn't actually quite "do what Foster recommends." While backing Dulles formally, Eisenhower, at Rockefeller's urging, hedged his bet by sending Rockefeller, Stassen, Robert Anderson, and Admiral Radford to Paris. Rockefeller took along to Paris several members of his staff and Possony. They were joined by George Pettee, a veteran of the Quantico Panel, who happened to be in town on other business. There is no direct evidence of which I am aware; but from the constitution of the Paris group it is possible, if not likely, that Eisenhower had in mind the Open Skies proposal as a contingency. It may be, even, that Eisenhower had quietly decided that he would make the proposal unless circumstances on the spot indicated otherwise.

Rockefeller was a hard man to repress, and his fencing with Dulles continued in Washington right down to the departure of the two groups for their respective posts in Europe. The fencing centered on the drafts of the president's brief talk to the American people on the evening of July 15 and his opening statement at the conference on July 18.

On Friday, July 8, Rockefeller included in the president's weekend reading two alternative drafts for possible use in Eisenhower's speech to the American people before his departure. On July 11 the drafts were sent to Dulles. Perhaps in response, Dulles dictated on July 13 the notes in Appendix J, extracted on page 47 above.

The second of the two speech drafts sent to Eisenhower and Dulles on July 8 and 11 was, in fact, designed as an opening speech at the summit (see Appendix K). I drafted it on June 20 after the Quantico sessions. Although quite different in tone and texture than Dulles', the point of this and other presummit drafts in which Rockefeller and I were involved was quite limited and specific: to foreshadow and, if possible, to commit the president to making concrete proposals, as opposed to Dulles' notion of his merely identifying areas for later negotiation by the foreign ministers. (For C. D. Jackson's account of the fencing over the drafts, see Appendix D.) Here, for example, are two key paragraphs from the June 20 draft which, in effect, translate the Quantico suggestions into operating presidential language:

> . . . I see no possibility of moving seriously toward the ending of the arms race until it is demonstrated as a matter of fact that an effective inspection system, which we all can trust, will actually work. This is the place to begin on the control of armaments; and we will make precise proposals to this effect. I see no possibility of moving seriously on the question of Germany until it is demonstrated as a matter of fact that free German elections can take place throughout all of Germany; and we will make precise proposals on this point as well.
>
> Both with respect to the control of armaments and with respect to the freeing of Germany the larger question is this: can we begin concretely and practically to create the underlying conditions for peace? This must include a much wider exchange of ideas, a much freer exchange of personal contacts, and higher levels of trade. In addition to our

central proposals on the control of armaments and on Germany, we are anxious to explore on a practical basis measures of this kind.

On this matter, Rockefeller won a limited but certainly not a decisive victory with the following passage in Eisenhower's opening statement at Geneva:

> Surprise attack has a capacity for destruction far beyond anything which man has yet known. So each of us deems it vital that there should be means to deter such attack. Perhaps, therefore, we should consider whether the problem of limitation of armament may not best be approached by seeking—as a first step—dependable ways to supervise and inspect military establishments, so that there can be no frightful surprises, whether by sudden attack or by secret violation of agreed restrictions. In this field nothing is more important than that we explore together the challenging and central problem of effective mutual inspection. Such a system is the foundation for real disarmament.

Thus, the Open Skies issue was alive but unsettled as the two parties went to work in Geneva and Paris.

While decorous but sterile formal diplomatic and informal social exchanges proceeded in Geneva on July 18–19, things were a bit livelier at the Hotel Crillon, where the rear echelon was quartered. Parker's chronology at the head of this chapter and Jackson's reconstructed narrative in Appendix D capture essentially what happened.

On the eighteenth Rockefeller, wasting no time, briefed Radford, Stassen, Anderson, and the rest of the Paris contingent on the Open Skies proposal.[28] Initially, Rockefeller made little progress, but, in the wake of an intervention by Possony, Radford firmly grasped the concept and approved it. Possony recalled for me on July 17, 1980, when I was drafting this chapter, his trepidation: here he was, a modest civilian in the Pentagon, with a quite rich Hungarian accent, intervening to educate the chairman of the Joint Chiefs of Staff. As Possony remembers, Radford responded by saying: "It's a good idea. Let me take it from here." By the night of the eighteenth Parker was able to set down the following memorandum for the record:

MEMO FOR RECORD (Meeting of 1030 hours, 18 July 1955)
Subject: Admiral Radford's Views on Proposal for Inspection
        Without Limitation of Arms

1. Admiral Radford indicated considerable interest in the proposal for mutual inspection of military installations as a first step in our efforts toward disarmament, without any concurrent attempt to limit or reduce force or arms levels.

2. He suggested that the U.S. should furnish the U.S.S.R. a list of our military installations which their representatives might visit and inspect, in return for a similar list of U.S.S.R. installations which U.S. representatives might visit and inspect. He pointed out that the Soviets are unlikely to accept such a proposal, but if they should, from a military viewpoint, it would be to the advantage of the U.S. to make such an agreement, since the Soviets already have most of the information they could obtain through such a privilege, whereas we have little or none.

3. He discussed specifically the question of mutual right to overfly the territory of the other nation, pointing out what an intelligence advantage this would have for the U.S. Ostensibly the overflight authority would be for the purpose of determining what installations each inspecting group desired to inspect in the territory of the other nation.

4. Admiral Radford is very strong in his opinion that the inspecting teams should consist of Soviets only for inspection of U.S., and U.S. only for inspection of U.S.S.R. He quoted difficulties in Korea in support of his view.

5. In summary, Admiral Radford feels that the U.S.S.R. would probably turn down a U.S. proposal for such an inspection agreement, or for an agreement to study such a system. It is his opinion that the U.S. will gain a decided public opinion advantage. If they accept, he feels it is an agreement we can accept, and one which will give the U.S. a decided intelligence advantage.

Something almost equally important happened later on the eighteenth which is best recounted in Parker's words in a letter to me of June 12, 1981:

> Our [NAR staff] game plan in Paris was to watch for the moment when the U.S. Delegation in Geneva ran out of ammunition. This moment came even earlier than we had anticipated. We had a staff level telephone conversation with Goodpaster late-evening (almost midnight as I remember) on Monday, July 18. I'm not sure now whether he initiated the call or me, probably the latter. We had an understanding with Andy that we in Paris would use him as our liaison in Geneva. Andy gave us the flavor of the opening day's exchanges, a sterile one as you recount, and painted a gloomy picture of the U.S. Delegation's prospects for injecting life in the proceedings. When we spoke of trying to be of some help in this respect by offering some input, he encouraged us, and we worked during the night . . . [The drafting on the night of July 18–19 was mainly done by Kintner and Possony.]

With Radford aboard, Goodpaster encouraging, and a night of staff work in hand, things moved swiftly on the morning of Tuesday the nineteenth. Stassen and Anderson rallied in support of the idea; and a statement was drafted for the president to use on the twenty-first, formally scheduled for disarmament discussions. Two messages were then dispatched to Geneva: one from Anderson and Radford to Dulles underlined the importance of the inspection issue; the other from Rockefeller to Goodpaster, sent at 1:15 P.M., contained the agreed draft statement for the president (full text in Appendix E), including this passage: "Inspection teams should also be free to overfly the territory of the nation being inspected, in order to determine by aerial observation the location and activity of military establishments in its territory and to make sure that none remains hidden." As the full text of that message makes clear, its proposal for providing information on the location of military establishments was less sweeping than that which Eisenhower, in fact, made on the twenty-first.

Later on the nineteenth Rockefeller and Stassen were ordered to Geneva, flying in a military aircraft. There was, apparently, no hotel space in Geneva that the American delegation could provide for Rockefeller's staff. Its members set up shop in Lausanne and commuted to Geneva in the final days of the conference.

On July 19–20, Alfred Gruenther, commanding general of the allied forces of NATO, was brought into the act from two distinct directions. On the nineteenth, Radford and Anderson appear to have sought him out to brief him on what might be afoot, perhaps on Eisenhower's instructions, perhaps on their own initiative. In the wake of breakfast with Eden on the twentieth, Eisenhower asked Radford and Gruenther to come to Geneva immediately and reported that Eden wanted Gruenther and the senior British officer at SHAPE, General Nevil Brownjohn, to discuss the proposal. There was a technical problem to be resolved here: how would the proposal for exchange of information on military establishments and mutual aerial inspection relate to the existing operation of the so-called Potsdam teams? That is, representatives of the Warsaw Pact were permitted to travel anywhere in West Germany while reciprocal privileges were granted military teams from NATO in East Germany.

In any case, Gruenther was in Geneva for the critical meeting early on the evening of Wednesday, July 20, described at the opening of Chapter 1. Given his close ties to Eisenhower and the latter's respect for him, Gruenther's supporting voice was undoubtedly important. Next to Gruenther, the other most influential supporter of the proposal, apart from Radford, was probably Andrew Goodpaster. Although only a colonel in rank, Goodpaster served as a personal aide to Eisenhower with the passion for anonymity commended to Franklin Roosevelt when the concept of presidential aides was proposed by the Brownlow Committee in 1936—a passion notably lacking in some who subsequently served in such posts. Goodpaster not only mobilized for the president information on military and foreign affairs but was also systematically asked for his views. His functions foreshadowed rather more closely those of the series of post-1961 special assistants for national security affairs than the functions of those who held that title in the Eisenhower administration. The latter were mainly engaged in managing a complex system of interagency committees. In a phrase of the man holding the post, he was a "neutral keeper of the machinery." Goodpaster had been at the final formal session of the Quantico Panel on June 9, fully understood the Open Skies proposal and the framework of thought that lay behind it, and had indicated his support to Eisenhower.

With all the relevant characters assembled, events unfolded on July 20−21 as described in Chapter 1. There was some difficulty in the drafting, which Eisenhower assigned to Stassen. Stassen appeared to resist the notion of exchanging blueprints of military establishments, but Rockefeller succeeded in restoring both elements in the Open Skies proposal. In a gracious letter of July 27, Stassen acknowledged Rockefeller's crucial role in the Open Skies initiative (see Appendix L).

On the evening of the twenty-first, after Eisenhower's presentation, Rockefeller and his staff celebrated with, among other things, a bucket of caviar; but Rockefeller found time to dispatch cables to all members of the Quantico Panel who were not with him in Geneva.

5. The Aftermath

As noted in Chapter 1, Eisenhower's Open Skies initiative was generally regarded as a great success: it was concrete and understandable; it seemed to open a possible door to arms control at a time when the reality of fusion weapons had heightened anxiety; it dramatized effectively the authentic desire of the United States to move toward peace; as a piece of gamesmanship it laid before Moscow a tough question that would have to be answered; and as the French premier Edgar Faure said, Eisenhower "scored the first great victory over scepticism."

In a roundup of reactions, the *New York Herald Tribune* reported on July 22:

> Both the Senate and House, in an outburst of bipartisan acclaim, today welcomed President Eisenhower's Big-Four proposal for exchanging complete military information as a bold but practical diplomatic move sure of proving America's own peaceful intentions and certain of testing those of the Russians.
>
> As word of the President's dramatic intervention at Geneva spread over Capitol Hill, individual Senators and Representatives of both parties had nothing but praise for the invitation to disarm. The tributes were another indication of the strong two-party support backing Mr. Eisenhower at Geneva.
>
> One of the first to acclaim the President's Geneva action was Sen. Lyndon B. Johnson, Tex. The Senate majority leader,

still hospitalized by the heart attack he suffered three weeks ago, hailed the Eisenhower proposal as "the daring, imaginative stroke for which a war-weary world has been waiting."

Bringing up a point that was frequently echoed elsewhere, Sen. Johnson said the President's gesture "will test the good faith of the Communists and separate the warmongers from the peacemakers. The American people yearn for peace— peace that will maintain their traditional freedoms."

And, in general, reactions in politically open societies were similarly positive, the public enjoying what was clearly a *coup de théâtre*, an element in short supply at diplomatic conferences, even at the summit. And, after a short delay, the Soviet press published the text of Eisenhower's proposal.

Approbation was, of course, by no means universal. Some of the more conservative Republican senators were clearly grumpy, as the *Washington Post* reported on July 23: William Knowland, Styles Bridges, and Eugene Millikin. Their dissidence stemmed in part from the fact that they had not been consulted. Indeed, no one in Washington was informed of the probability of the president's initiative until early in the morning of July 21 Geneva time (see Appendix A). Given the time difference, they could, at best, have known about it only shortly before it was on the wire service ticker tapes. Senator Joseph McCarthy was openly hostile, but his day had passed by July 1955.

From a quite different perspective, James Reston of the *New York Times* was explicitly critical. Clearly the proposal had caught him by surprise. His dispatch from Geneva of July 20 portrayed accurately, no doubt from an authoritative source, the Geneva strategy as Dulles had initially defined it and which Eisenhower had formally approved over Rockefeller's objection before departure for Geneva:[29]

> The President, however, is doing precisely what he told his associates here Saturday night that he was going to do. . . .

. . . the President agreed with Mr. Dulles and the others that this was not the time or the place to try to get down to details. He insisted this was the place to encourage the new conciliatory line of the Soviet leaders and to try to establish personal relationships that would pay off in the later stages when the East and West were ready for detailed negotiations.

He has stuck to that line all week. . . .

Once in contact with the British, Soviet and French leaders, . . . he has shunned specifics like the plague and his only interventions in the debate today were general exhortations for everybody to get together.

Later in the same dispatch Reston noted the somewhat disconcerting arrival of the Paris contingent, finding different, specific reasons for the presence of each, including this for Gruenther:

. . . he wanted General Gruenther here for the simple reason that he likes him and wanted to play bridge with him tonight.

Nobody quite believes the Gruenther story, but it's true.

His July 21 dispatch (headed "Change in Parley Course") was probably the most critical account of Eisenhower's initiative to appear in the Western press:

The Big Four conference is declining fast. What was advertised for weeks as a realistic private discussion of conflicting national interests, and started this week as a determined demonstration of international chumminess, developed today into a propaganda battle between the United States and the Soviet Union.

There is nothing new about this so far as the Russians are concerned. They have been making propaganda since Monday.

The new thing is that President Eisenhower joined the propaganda parade today with a vengeance. He produced the only new dramatic proposal of the week. He suggested that the United States and the Soviet Union let each other know everything about each other's defense establishments. He proposed, further, that they, the Russians, fly all over the United States photographing our military establishments and that they let us do the same in the Soviet Union.

This was the surprise of the conference for a variety of reasons. In the first place it was generally regarded as unrealistic. As President Eisenhower himself said yesterday, the Soviet Union already knows almost everything it needs to know about United States defense arrangements. The Soviet leaders do not need to hand over their defense blueprints and let United States aviators photograph their country to find out what the United States is doing.

Second, it is illegal under United States laws. Nobody, for example, is allowed to fly over the atomic energy projects in Savannah River, S.C.; Oak Ridge, Tenn.; Hanford, Wash.; or Los Alomos [*sic*], N.M.

Third, in the light of these facts it seemed to other Western delegates to be a proposal like the Soviet proposal for the destruction of all atomic bombs and the dismantling of Allied air bases, which the other side knew in advance had no chance of being accepted.

Fourth—and this was the greatest surprise of all—the idea of exchanging defense blueprints and aerial photographs with Moscow, forbidden under United States law, apparently was not explored in any detail, if at all, with Congressional leaders, who make the laws.

Everybody in the United States delegation here knew the President was going to make an important disarmament speech. Photographers were alerted ahead of time for the briefing. Plans were made to reproduce and publicize his remarks.

The idea of exchanging "defense blueprints" with the Soviet Union and taking aerial photographs of the United States and Soviet defense establishments had been discussed casually here in private meetings, but it apparently was not in the draft of the speech General Eisenhower took with him to the Palace of Nations this afternoon.

When Marshal Nikolai A. Bulganin, Soviet Premier, started talking about the Soviet ideas of disarmament, however,

President Eisenhower apparently decided to spring his "blueprint" and aerial photograph ideas.

This, of course, he had every right to do. He is the President of the United States, its Chief Executive and Commander in Chief of its armed forces. But his proposal was not in keeping with the principles or the tactics he has recommended ever since he arrived at the summit.

The President's contention all week has been that this was a conference not for orations but for discussions, not for controversial details but for general principles, not for emphasizing the things that divide "the four," but for emphasizing the things that unite them.

The United States delegation at the summit has been politely annoyed by the tendency of the British and French to propose specific plans that had little chance of careful discussion, let alone negotiations, in Geneva.

The United States delegates have been pointing to the President's own tactics here this week as a model of how to act at a short conference of this kind. He has been full of goodwill toward everybody. He has been courting the Russians one by one, so much so that they have been saying privately here for the last two days that they are convinced there will never be a war so long as he is President.

This was the traditional Eisenhower operating on his own, applying to international politics the personal habits that elevated him to the top in the army and finally to the summit of United States political life.

Yesterday, however, a new flock of advisers arrived at the summit from Washington—Admiral Arthur W. Radford, chairman of the Joint Chiefs of Staff, Harold E. Stassen, disarmament assistant, and Nelson A. Rockefeller, White House propaganda chief. The President has been in conference with them ever since.

Whether they persuaded him to change his tactics or whether one or another of them merely threw out ideas he accepted was still a matter of speculation here tonight.

The fact is, however, that he changed his line. He is still saying that a new spirit and good faith may dissolve the contradictory East-West policies on German unity and European security but today's barrage of Soviet propaganda followed by President Eisenhower's improvisations have not improved the outlook.

There was a good deal of legitimate argument in Reston's July 21 dispatch, although one can't help feeling he was somewhat put out because, as a reporter, he had been misled unwittingly by his Geneva sources.

Eisenhower, in fact, was deadly serious about the Open Skies proposal, and his seriousness transcended Radford's perception that, if accepted, it would provide a net intelligence advantage for the United States. As Eisenhower had said to Dulles on July 6 (see above, p. 46), he regarded the concept as "an idea that might open a tiny gate in the disarmament fence." And, like most serious professional military men who had lived through the transition from conventional to nuclear arms, he understood with authentic horror the meaning of the quantum jump in the powers of destruction. In a discussion about the Atoms for Peace proposal on January 16, 1954, Eisenhower spoke in ways which clearly foreshadow the reasons for both his skepticism of the Soviet fixed post inspection scheme of May 10, 1955, and the depth of his interest in mutual aerial inspection:

> 1. Meeting with the President on atomic disarmament between State and Defense. Foster Dulles, Beedle Smith, Roger Kyes, Admiral Davis, Lewis Strauss. No problems.
> President very forthright and forceful making it all simple and clear, his central point being—The atomic weapon is the first weapon which ever really scared America, because for the first time American industry, which won previous world wars, could be crippled before war started. Therefore, if the atomic weapon could be completely outlawed, he would be for it, even though this would leave Russia with vast conventional superiority, because we could make up the difference through our industry so long as we were immune to destructive attack. However, effective outlawing of atomic weapons is impossible, because (a) we cannot believe the

Soviets, (b) adequate inspection and control is impossible. If the Swiss and the Swedes cannot inspect North Korea, how can we inspect USSR? Therefore, argument is academic. However, let's go ahead with the atom-for-peace proposal, and if the Soviets wish to talk about atomic disarmament we will listen.[30]

In the wake of his Geneva proposal, Eisenhower knew his problem did not lie with the Senate conservatives or the *New York Times*. It lay with the Soviet leaders. He accepted the Soviet fixed post proposal if it were combined with Open Skies; and he concentrated all his powers of persuasion in the final phase of the conference on Khrushchev, who had, in the end, agreed that the Soviet government would not "kick the idea out the window" but study it carefully, despite his (Khrushchev's) strong reservations.[31] Eisenhower's personal secretary, Mrs. Whitman, described to me, in the course of writing this volume, a final desperate effort on July 23 after the formal adjournment. Eisenhower swept up Charles Bohlen, then ambassador to Moscow and Eisenhower's interpreter at the conference, and rushed down the corridors of the Palais des Nations to the Soviet delegation offices for one more try. The Soviet leaders had just departed.

Nevertheless, the U.S. government proceeded to follow up on the Open Skies initiative in a thoroughly professional way. At Geneva the various disarmament proposals of the four governments were referred to the United Nations Disarmament Commission, but the issue was also placed on the agenda of the meeting of the four foreign ministers scheduled for later in the year. The U.N. commission met from August 29 to October 7. Stassen presented a detailed version of Open Skies, including in his package the Soviet proposal for ground observers. On August 18, while the commission was at work, Bulganin sent a letter to Eisenhower formally confirming a position he had taken on August 4 when addressing the Supreme Soviet. Open Skies was set aside on three grounds:

1. The U.S. and the U.S.S.R. were so vast that aerial inspection would not preclude concealment.

2. It did not provide for aerial inspection of troops and installations outside the two countries.

3. The U.S. proposals as a whole did not provide for prompt arms reductions.

Politely phrased, in the Spirit of Geneva as it was then called, the Bulganin letter did not rule out the possibility of mutual aerial inspection playing an ultimate role in arms control proposals; but it flatly rejected Eisenhower's fundamental proposition, that is, arms control measures required as a prior condition confidence that verification was possible and reliable. Bulganin's key passage was the following: "All this shows that the problem of aerial photography is not a question which, under present conditions, would lead to effective progress toward insuring security of states and successful accomplishment of disarmament."

Before Eisenhower could reply, he suffered a heart attack on September 24. He sent an interim response on October 11. The correspondence continued decorously but without issue into 1956, involving Germany and other matters including the Soviet offer of a bilateral Treaty of Friendship and Cooperation between the U.S. and U.S.S.R., offered on January 23, 1956, rejected with impeccable politeness on January 28.

For our limited purposes, the simple fact is that Open Skies was rejected by Bulganin, and his rejection was bluntly confirmed by Molotov at the sterile meeting of the foreign ministers which took place at Geneva from October 27 to November 16, 1955. Support for Open Skies (along with various other disarmament proposals) at the U.N. General Assembly gave little comfort to those who, like Eisenhower, took arms control seriously and saw in the Open Skies scheme a potential stabilizing device in a nuclear age which might, indeed, open the way for serious arms control agreements. Diplomacy having failed, aerial inspection was left to the intelligence services and the march of technology, yielding in the

1960s a tacit, but still fragile, common-law agreement that mutual satellite photography would be tolerated.

The foreign ministers' meeting in the autumn of 1955 was equally and even more unambiguously sterile on the issue of Germany, while events in the Middle East and other parts of the developing regions stirred rising anxiety in Washington and Western Europe. It was increasingly clear that the Geneva summit of July 1955 had been, from the Soviet point of view, part of a strategy for quieting the West, increasing, if possible, tensions between the United States and its Western European partners, and pursuing an activist anti-Western strategy in the developing regions. The Council on Foreign Relations volume, *The United States in World Affairs, 1955*, published early in the next year, accurately summarized the state of affairs with a chapter entitled "Ascent and Descent of the 'Summit.'"

While formal U.S. diplomacy plodded its way to the end of the year with increasing disappointment, Rockefeller, who shared the Quantico Panel's view that the summit should be regarded as a test of Soviet intentions, drew immediately from the Soviet performance at Geneva the conclusion that peace was not about to break out and that the United States should begin to bestir itself. He gained Eisenhower's permission to mount a second Quantico Panel to take fundamental stock of the nation's military and political position on the world scene and to propose long-term policies to meet its weaknesses. The result is accurately described by James Desmond:

> The second Quantico conference was held September 25th to 29th. Again all the panelists were top men in their fields and in the government, and again all had to get security clearance to give them access to the top-secret material that comprised the working papers for the studies. But unlike the first meeting, which was concerned solely with preparing for Geneva, the later panel gave only incidental thought to the Foreign Ministers' Conference, then being

planned by the State Department, and spread its concerns over nearly all aspects of national and international affairs. Although some ideas generated at Quantico II went into the State Department hopper for use at the Foreign Ministers' meeting, the complete, 41-page, unanimous report of the panel wasn't published until December when Nelson was clearing up his desk to resign. Its circulation was restricted to government officials qualified to receive classified material.

The Quantico II report was never acted on as a whole, perhaps because of its cost—a whopping $18 billion over six years to build up our military and economic strength around the world—but many of its concepts have since filtered into our policy. As an example, one may cite President Kennedy's buildup of conventional military forces to fight less-than-nuclear wars. The concept became commonplace by the 1960's, but in 1955, despite the lesson of the Korean War, our military strategy was keyed almost wholly to atomic deterrence. The panel was clearly ahead of its time in this and other matters.

The report also enunciated four precepts that Rockefeller continues to regard as the cornerstones of foreign policy. These call for: full disclosure of the dangers confronting the country to rally the national will behind the government; military spending on whatever scale is necessary to make sure our defense never becomes second best; economic aid to build up the free countries so they can eventually contribute to the defense effort around the world; and constant pressure on the Communists to unmask the true intentions behind their propaganda and so-called aid programs. As a corollary to the military buildup, Rockefeller, both as Special Assistant and as Governor of New York, has stressed the overriding importance of an adequate civilian defense program to impress on the Russians that our people will fight if forced to war.[32]

Although Rockefeller initially enlisted Millikan and me to help organize Quantico II, I did not actually participate in the meeting for a reason hard to understand outside the context of Washington in the 1950s. I held, at the time, a top secret clearance from one Washington agency, valid throughout Washington; and I continued to hold it. Quantico II required, however, further higher clearances since it dealt in detail with certain sensitive military issues. Those granting the clearances turned down two of Rockefeller's nominees for the panel, including me, not on security grounds but because we were judged "controversial." This was part of a general harassing campaign against Rockefeller in the latter months of 1955 as he evoked the enmity, not only of Dulles, but also of the powerful members of the administration who regarded him as a dangerous "big spender"—notably George Humphrey, Charles Wilson, and Rockefeller's old sparring partner, Herbert Hoover, Jr., undersecretary of state.

As 1955 wound down, Rockefeller was increasingly convinced he would have to resign. His budgetary proposals led Secretary of Defense Wilson to withdraw an offer for Rockefeller to take over as his deputy. But Rockefeller definitely made up his mind to resign after an hour's session on December 5 at Gettysburg, where Eisenhower was recuperating. The president clearly indicated that he would not act to implement the Quantico II budget recommendations. Reporting this conversation to me shortly thereafter at lunch in the MIT Faculty Club, Rockefeller noted that he found Eisenhower so restless, confined to Gettysburg, that he was sure he would run again in 1956. He also expressed a conclusion he conveyed to a good many others at that time: he would never again serve in Washington except as an elected official, a decision he was to violate by accepting the appointment in 1974 as vice-president.

Rockefeller evidently judged his best option was to challenge Averell Harriman as governor of New York in 1958, but he was not about to waste 1956 and 1957. Using as a base the Rockefeller Brothers Fund, over which he came to preside in 1956, he organized, with the active support of his brothers, a large-scale, public version of Quantico II, widened in scope to include education and domestic economic problems. There were six panels in all, involving almost a hundred substantive figures in American life, from both political parties: businessmen and labor leaders, foundation officials and academics, scientists and retired military men, lawyers and at least one cleric (James Pike). From the White House, Andrew Goodpaster participated. The secretariat was headed by Henry Kissinger, whom Rockefeller came to know through the Quantico II exercise. Here was the American establishment in its heyday.

The panel reports were influential to a degree in shaping policy in the late 1950s, but they were more strongly reflected in the party platforms of 1960 and in Kennedy's policy in the early 1960s. Their influence derived from two sources. First, timing was right. The launching of the first Sputnik by the Soviet Union on October 4, 1957, galvanized the country with a sense that the United States was, in some fundamental sense, falling behind the Soviet Union. In the wake of Sputnik, Rockefeller rushed to bring the interim conclusions of Panel II to Eisenhower's attention, publishing the report as a whole early in 1958 as *International Security: The Military Aspect.* The conclusions of Panel II constituted a thoroughly professional attack on the adequacy of Eisenhower's military policy and his budget. Second, and more profoundly, for reasons suggested below, a conviction gathered momentum among the leaders of American society during Eisenhower's second term that, over a wide front, the nation was not dealing adequately with its military, diplomatic, and domestic problems. The panel reports were part of a process of which the Rockefeller Brothers Fund enterprise was only one component.

So far as military policy was concerned, there had spread, by a curious and subtle process, both a knowledge of the essential military facts and a consensus on the directions in which the administration's policy ought to be changed. Leading businessmen, scientists, labor leaders, lawyers, foundation officers, soldiers, journalists, professors, and unemployed politicians of both parties had begun to acquire a sufficiently firm and confident grasp on the facts to challenge the administration's policy and to formulate an alternative.

How did this come about? First, a considerable number of citizens had been drawn into advisory groups by the government on particular national security questions and given access to at least a portion of the evidence available on the relative military positions of the United States and the Soviet Union. These groups systematically emerged from their tasks urging an enlarged American effort. They derived from the facts recommendations for policy different from those drawn by the highest administration officials. Second, by various devices—ranging from congressional hearings to the annual strategy seminars at the army, navy, and air war colleges—the three services made available estimates of the situation and recommendations for policy at variance with the administration's official view. No one of these occasions or devices was in itself decisive, but they had a cumulative effect within the circle of those outside the government deeply concerned with security affairs. Third, the Council on Foreign Relations in New York kept a substantial group of men from this circle quite professionally briefed in military and foreign policy matters; and, to a degree, similar independent examinations of military policy were being conducted at universities and elsewhere throughout the nation. Finally, of course, the normal process of a free politics and a free journalism had exposed facts and issues for debate which, while ineffective in themselves in causing a shift in national policy, had helped create a climate of latent uneasiness which the Soviet launching of an earth satellite appeared to justify. The Symington hearings of 1956 played, for example, an important preparatory role in the post-Sputnik military crises.

In different ways these converging processes came to a

head in the Gaither Report and in the Rockefeller Panel Report II. From press accounts it would appear that those who prepared the Gaither Report had been assembled in the summer of 1957 to examine the question of whether the nation should invest large resources in the construction of shelters which would protect its citizens against fallout in case of nuclear attack. As is often the case with men engaged on a specific problem in a complex general context, their first impulse was to conclude that the narrow question could be answered only if placed in a broader context. They sought a total picture of the existing and foreseeable Soviet threat and of American dispositions, current and prospective, to meet that threat; and they managed to act on this impulse and brought the camel into the tent.

Thus, by early October 1957, they had assembled from official sources an estimate of the total military situation and an array of recommendations for national security policy as a whole alternative to those on which the nation had been operating. The Gaither Report recommended a radical increase in military expenditure in a good many directions, and it challenged the administration view that the United States could maintain effective deterrence of Soviet military strength at the existing level and organization of the nation's military effort. In the wake of the launching of the second Soviet earth satellite, this view was laid before the National Security Council, an occasion of some historical moment since it represented in effect a charge by one wing of the Republican party (symbolized, for example, by Robert Lovett, John McCloy, and William Foster) that those in command had not met adequately their first responsibility to the nation over the previous several years.

The substance of the consensus which had been developed on military policy in the two previous years was published shortly thereafter in the Rockefeller Panel Report II. Its conclusions, summarized in Note 33, reflect the precision with which a consensus had been reached outside the government on issues normally inaccessible to the democratic process unless the executive branch makes them so.[33]

Point by point, the Rockefeller Panel Report II was a public rejection of the Great Equation of 1953—involving primary reliance on nuclear deterrence—and the specific policies which the Eisenhower administration had built upon it over the previous five years. The report rejected the notion that a healthy, recognizably American society required for the maintenance of its institutions a rigid limitation of budgetary expenditures. It rejected the concept that an ability to retaliate with nuclear weapons was a sufficient deterrent to Soviet strength. It rejected the continued denial to NATO of information about nuclear weapons and the weapons themselves. It rejected the notion that existing dispositions were sufficient to maintain American retaliatory power over the foreseeable future. It rejected the pattern of administration which had emerged during the previous five years in the Department of Defense, including the priority for and methods of handling research and development.

The clarity and detail with which these positions were articulated and the ability to get virtual unanimity on them in a group as diverse as the almost fifty signers of the Panel II report are to be understood only in the light of the process which had preceded that report over the previous three years.

In a sense, a representative group of leaders from both political parties had formed a kind of shadow cabinet in opposition. With the help of experts inside and outside the government, they had done their homework on the nation's security problem; and they were able to persuade a kind of informal senate, made up of leaders from a wide range of American private institutions, to back this alternative program against the president. It is doubtful that unanimity around anything like such a program could have been achieved without the Soviet launching of the earth satellites, but the ground was well laid. There was already a substantial body of highly responsible American citizens prepared to commit themselves to an alternative program when the demonstration of Soviet capabilities was made.

It was, once again, the existence of a massive body of evidence which had been carefully analyzed before the event which permitted a unanimous report to emerge from Senator Johnson's Preparedness Subcommittee in the Senate on January 7, 1958, with its fourteen-point program.

There was a similar emergence of consensus in other fields. Something clearly had to be done about the economy, which, in Eisenhower's phrase, "sputtered" during his second term, with recurrent recessions, low average growth, an emerging element of wage-push inflation, and a gold outflow reflecting a lag in U.S. productivity increase relative to Western Europe and Japan. There was similar soul-searching about the educational system, public services, and the beginnings of a consciousness that the problems of race were rising rapidly on the national agenda. And in foreign policy the concern about the military balance with the Soviet Union was matched, among a good many, by gathering awareness that we had no adequate policy to deal constructively with the developing regions—a process to be analyzed in the next (fifth) book of this series. In one way or another, Kennedy gathered all this under the spacious tent of "Let's get this country moving again" in 1960. But Nixon, mainly on his own but, in part, also because of an election-year deal with Rockefeller, moved toward the new consensus.

It was clearly what Moscow was up to in the post–Geneva summit period which most substantially stirred the nation to take stock and look in new policy directions. As noted earlier (see pp. 14–22), Soviet strategy in the wake of Stalin's death came to focus on efforts to expand its power in the developing regions and on the buildup of its military capacity, notably with respect to missiles with fusion warheads.

The Egyptian arms deal of 1955, successfully leapfrogging the Baghdad Pact, opened a phase of rolling crisis in relations between the Soviet Union and the West; but it was the related nationalization of the Suez Canal and the subsequent abortive Anglo-French effort to gain control of the canal which raised the curtain on the new period. Eisenhower wrote to a friend on November 18, 1957: "'Since July 25th of 1956, when Nasser announced the nationalization of Suez, I cannot remember a day that has not brought its major or minor crisis.' Crisis has now become 'normalcy.'"[34] And that was the way it was to be down to the end of his term. The major crises of the period included Sputnik and its shock waves within the Atlantic Alliance as well as at home, starting in October 1957; Lebanon-Jordan (May–August 1958); Quemoy-Matsu (August–October 1958); the revival of war in Indochina, starting in 1958; the Soviet threat of a treaty with East Germany, terminating allied rights in Berlin, starting with a statement by Khrushchev on November 10, 1958; the emergence of Castro as a Communist closely allied to Moscow, in 1959; the breakup of the Paris summit over the U-2 incident, May 1960; and the revolt in the Congo and the struggle for its leadership, starting in July 1960. Aside from the launching of Sputnik, the related Berlin ultimatum, and the U-2 crisis, the Soviet role in these crises was marginal but significant. The Soviet leadership perceived correctly that the developing regions were in a volatile state and set out to exploit systematically the opportunities that volatility offered to diminish the power of the West and to expand its own influence.

The nuclear question interwove that process in a quite particular way, notably after the launching of a Soviet ICBM in August 1957 and the first Sputnik on October 4. Khrushchev encouraged the view that the Soviet ICBM capability was greater than it was; and this image was the backdrop to the Moscow conference, in November 1957, of the leaders of the twelve Communist parties that had achieved control over nation-states. Mao spoke for the mood of that meeting:

> The superiority of the anti-imperialist forces over the im-
> perialist forces . . . has expressed itself in even more con-

centrated form and reached unprecedented heights with the Soviet Union's launching of the artificial satellites. . . . That is why we say that this is a new turning point in the international situation. . . .[35]

This was the perspective which inspired the Communist adventures which gathered momentum in Southeast Asia, the Congo, and the Caribbean and which lay behind Khrushchev's effort to translate the image of Soviet nuclear superiority into control over Berlin.

It was, of course, not quite that simple. The somewhat euphoric November 1957 meeting in Moscow also set in motion tensions between Moscow and Peking which, between January and April 1958, brought on a definitive break over the nuclear question.[36] Moscow's differences with Peking over nuclear matters, including the appropriate degree of risk to assume in Communist expansionist adventures, do not concern us here, but they help account for Khrushchev's maintenance of a continuing line of communication with the United States, his 1959 visit, and his efforts to keep things relatively quiet with Western Europe while he undermined its position in Africa and elsewhere.

What is clear in retrospect is that a good deal of the pressure on the West which generated in the period 1958–1960, presenting Kennedy with a rather formidable agenda of international troubles, stemmed from the Soviet launching of the first space satellite.

The U-2 did not cover enough of the Soviet Union to permit the U.S. government to be sure that Khrushchev's purposeful posturing about the Soviet ICBM capability was grossly exaggerated. As Paul Worthman observes (see Note 3), the limitations of the U-2 effort are "almost shocking." Khrushchev was prepared to use to the hilt the image of the new Soviet nuclear delivery capacity, but he was under no illusion that his strength had surpassed that of the United States or—a quite distinct matter—had made war with the

United States an acceptable risk. Moreover, his chosen arena for the application of Soviet nuclear leverage was Europe rather than Asia. He had real MRBM's and IRBM's targeted on Western Europe rather than the fictitious ICBM's allegedly targeted on the United States.

The simple fact is that Moscow decided in 1957 not to produce ICBM's on a large scale until a more efficient model was available; but the Soviet leadership also decided that it would proceed to project to the world, for political and psychological purposes, the image of a rapidly growing, even massive ICBM capability. As the best historians of this strategy state:

> Beginning in the late summer of 1957, the Soviet leaders, and chiefly Khrushchev, undertook to deceive the West regarding their strategic capabilities. The maneuver is remarkable for its deliberate and systematic character and for the relative consistency with which it was executed over a period of four years.[37]

The ability of Moscow to conceal its military dispositions made this exercise conceivable. The character of the Western press and competitive American politics completed the conditions for making the exercise viable. Khrushchev was, of course, aware of the U-2 flights from 1956; but he did not think the limited U-2 routes would reveal how few ICBM's were, in fact, emplaced.

The first generation of Soviet ICBM's was clumsy. And a massive missile production effort would have interfered with the priority Khrushchev attached to rapid agricultural and industrial growth. Technology and economics argued for a delayed deployment of more efficient ICBM's while secrecy offered the possibility of deception.

The upshot was that by 1961—four years after Sputnik— only a "handful" of Soviet ICBM's had actually been deployed.[38] But the upshot was also that, as of 1960, most of the world's citizens believed that the Soviet Union had outstripped the United States in strategic nuclear capabilities.

In August 1960 the United States Information Agency concluded:

> While sophisticated political and press opinion tends to regard the current military situation as one of nuclear stalemate in which neither of the two super-powers has any material advantage over the other, the more impressionistic popular opinion has seemingly concluded from Soviet boasts of superiority and American admissions of a temporary "missile gap" that the United States is not only currently militarily inferior to the USSR but will continue to be so for the next decade or two as well.[39]

In early 1960, public opinion polls in five Western European countries showed that the following percentages of people believed the U.S.S.R. to be ahead of the United States in military strength: Great Britain, 59; West Germany, 47; Norway, 45; France, 37; Italy, 32. Only in Italy did a higher percentage believe that the U.S. was ahead.[40] A good deal of the anxiety in the West and the high hopes generated in the Communist world could have been avoided if the United States had launched the first earth satellite, as it was quite capable of doing before the end of 1956.

The pre-Sputnik American space program was a limited affair, dominated by scientific rather than psychological and political considerations. On July 29, 1955, Eisenhower announced that the United States would undertake to orbit a satellite in connection with the International Geophysical Year—an eighteen-month period starting July 1, 1957, in which scientists would collaborate on a worldwide basis to advance knowledge of the earth and its environment.

Eisenhower notes (not quite accurately) that there was no appreciation in the United States government that the launching of the first Sputnik would have a major psychological and political effect;[41] and there was, objectively, no reason for surprise that the Soviet Union might launch the first satellite. The Soviets had made clear as early as April 1955 that they were working on a satellite; at an international meeting in June 1957, their scientists reminded their colleagues of their intention; and as early as November 1956 the American intelligence services estimated that a Soviet satellite could be launched after November 1957. When it was discovered in mid 1956 that the Jupiter booster had the capacity to launch a satellite before the end of the year, the military were divided but on balance wished to avoid diverting those at work on military missiles. The scientists saw no reason to alter the Vanguard plan or contaminate their enterprise with a sinister military connection. Only a few sensed the emotions that would be stirred in observing for the first time a man-made object twinkling in orbit beyond the earth's atmosphere. Among them was Nelson Rockefeller. In May 1955, when the issue of a Jupiter or Vanguard missile for the first satellite launch was argued before the NSC, he circulated a memorandum throughout the government as well as to the members of the council which included the following:

> I am impressed by the costly consequences of allowing the Russian initiative to outrun ours through an achievement that will symbolize scientific and technological advancement to people everywhere. The stake of prestige that is involved makes this a race we cannot afford to lose.[42]

Rockefeller's advice was not taken. The NSC approved the Vanguard plan on the condition that it not interfere with urgent work on military missiles. The Soviets proceeded with a space program squarely based on military missiles.

6. Some Reflections

The story of Eisenhower's Open Skies proposal of July 21, 1955, and its aftermath poses, among others, four issues of substance. Three remain of contemporary relevance; one is of some historical interest but is perhaps also relevant by analogy to experience with the U.S.-Soviet arms balance in the 1970s. The issues are:

1. The role of mutual aerial inspection in U.S.-Soviet relations.

2. The problems inherent in the relations between the White House staff and the rest of the federal bureaucracy, notably the Department of State.

3. The problem of generating new ideas in a big bureaucracy.

4. The extent to which Eisenhower's failure to react vigorously to Soviet intentions, as revealed at the summit of 1955 and at the subsequent foreign ministers' meeting of October–November, contributed to the gathering crises of the late 1950s. Put another way, was the tense and dangerous phase in U.S.-Soviet relations in the six years from, say, the nationalization of the Suez Canal to the Cuba missile crisis avoidable?

Eisenhower's presentation of the Open Skies proposal in Geneva was certainly, in part, a political and psychological act. It was meant to be, and it was both praised and criticized as such. It was also a proposal which, if rejected, would make unilateral photographic reconnaissance more justifiable. And, from the perspective of Quantico I, it was part of a test of Soviet intentions. But it also raised a fundamental and serious question: to what extent is mutual knowledge of military forces and dispositions of net advantage to both sides in a nuclear age? Despite Khrushchev's quick, understandable brush-off of Open Skies as an intelligence-gathering scheme of palpable net advantage to the West, there is considerable evidence that the Soviet government debated the matter seriously and over a considerable period of time, for Eisenhower's view that the proposal was, in the end, in the Soviet interest was correct in a longer-run perspective (see p. 9, above).

In the course of Bulganin's correct but sterile exchanges with Eisenhower in the wake of the summit, elements in that inner Soviet debate emerged and not always consistently. For example, Bulganin, on one occasion, evokes the danger that mutual aerial inspection would lead to unjustified complacency; on another, he considered the danger of heightened military competition:

> Finally, it is impossible not to stop and think about what would happen if we occupy ourselves with the questions of aerial photography and the exchange of military information without taking effective measures for reduction of armaments and prohibition of atomic weapons.
>
> I have apprehensions which I cannot help but share with you. Would not such a situation lead to the weakening of vigilance toward the still existing threat of violation of the peace generated by the arms race?
>
> It seems to us that in the present international situation and, moreover, under conditions of a completely unrestricted armaments race, the carrying out of such flights would not only fail to free the peoples from the fear of a new war, but on the contrary would intensify that fear and

mutual suspicion. Judge for yourself, Mr. President: what would the military leaders of your country do if it were reported to them that the aerophotography showed that your neighbor had more airfields? To be sure, they would order an immediate increase in the number of their own airfields. Naturally, our military leaders would do the same in a similar case. It is not difficult to understand that the result would be a further intensification of the armaments race.[43]

One can be quite sure that there were a good many papers written and committee meetings held on Open Skies in Moscow. Undoubtedly, there were those who argued, simply, that the Soviet Union enjoyed a relative intelligence advantage in dealing with an adversary whose open society provided, through congressional hearings, professional journals, academic symposia, Soviet agents, etc., such a massive and rich flow of military information. And they asked, as Khrushchev had from the beginning in Geneva, why the Soviet Union should surrender or radically reduce that advantage.

Others almost certainly argued a narrower, operational point: greater secrecy permitted the Soviet Union to pretend to greater military strength than actually existed, and this was both a deterrent to its adversaries and a pillar of support for its diplomacy. In the wake of the launching of the first Sputnik, with its astonishing and perhaps unanticipated global reaction, this argument no doubt gained ground. It is wholly understandable that, under such circumstances, Khrushchev was not anxious for the U.S. and the world generally to learn that his ICBM capability was much less than his posturing suggested; and it is not surprising that during this period of deception the Soviet Union would seek to shoot down a U-2 on the first occasion its antiaircraft capabilities permitted it to do so.

There were, no doubt, others who understood the three fundamental arguments on the other side:

1. No serious arms control agreement was possible without reliable inspection, and aerial inspection was less intrusive

than serious inspection (not fixed control points) on the ground.

2. Even without arms control agreements, mutual aerial inspection provided a means for avoiding excessive U.S. reactions to Soviet military strength and dispositions based on ignorance and the fear that ignorance induced in a nuclear age that inherently carried with it mortal danger to both sides.

3. Satellite photography provided a great deal of useful intelligence information beyond the territories of the two superpowers; and, as Sino-Soviet relations progressively deteriorated from early 1958 forward, Moscow, no doubt, was particularly interested in photographing China regularly.

Views on the first two of these propositions were temperately exchanged between U.S. and Soviet officials, scientists, and others on many occasions in the late 1950s and early 1960s. I was involved in one such set of exchanges at a Pugwash meeting in Moscow in December 1960, with participants from fifteen countries.

The formal position of the Soviet participants was quite clear: the degree of inspection should be proportioned to the degree of disarmament agreement. On both formal and informal occasions, some Americans present argued that a lack of information was inherently destabilizing in a nuclear age and that even limited arms control agreements required a high degree of confidence in their inspection provisions. If a government did not know what its potential adversary was up to, it had, for the most primitive security reasons, to assume the worst. In the course of a formal bilateral exchange of views between the U.S. and Soviet participants, at the close of the general session, Amrom Katz of RAND engagingly made a case for the pacifying effects of the U-2 and the destabilizing effects of its shooting down:

> About the U-2, much has already been said. Let me say only the following—it is quite clear by now that Mr. Khrushchev and our Soviet colleagues knew much more about

the U-2 during its entire history than did anyone sitting on the American side of the table. Did the U-2 fly over the Soviet Union for four years? Apparently.

Which U-2 flights did the Soviets more damage by their standards, the U-2's which flew over and returned safely, or the U-2 which they shot down? Clearly it must be the U-2 that returned, not the one that was shot down.

Yet I must point out that during this entire period the Soviet Union was engaged in serious negotiation and friendly conversation, and the spirit of Camp David was flying almost as high as the reputed height at which the U-2's flew. There is only one question I have then. Why did the Soviets shoot down the U-2 and spoil this nice situation and end this era of good will?[44]

The joke was too good not to be appreciated by the Soviet delegates, the point too sharp to be accepted. The chief of the Soviet delegation replied, in effect, that the U.S.S.R. had to have irrefutable proof of the flights to force the issue of their illegitimacy and, therefore, had to shoot one down at the first opportunity, meanwhile remaining silent.

In private conversations it was quite clear that some of the Soviet participants fully understood the case we were making and, in retrospect, it seems possible that they knew of and feared the playback effects on U.S. military policy of Khrushchev's propaganda projection of a Soviet ICBM capability far beyond reality. In addition, they may well have been conscious that Khrushchev's boasting generated pressures on the Soviet government from within the Communist camp to press harder against U.S. interests than was prudent from Moscow's point of view. I doubt if F. M. Cornford's minor classic, *Microcosmographia Academica*, was widely read in Moscow in the late 1950s; but one of its observations aptly matches one aspect of Khrushchev's ICBM deception: "Propaganda . . . [is] that branch of the art of lying which consists in very nearly deceiving your friends without quite deceiving your enemies."[45] In any case, some Soviet scientists and officials of the period avoided exaggerated claims of Soviet military progress and addressed the issues of arms control with evident seriousness. I do not know the weight given the judgment and advice of our more thoughtful Soviet Pugwash interlocutors in the decision finally made by the Soviet Union to accept as common law mutual satellite photography; but I can vouch for the fact that a number of Soviet officials and scientists fully understood the potentially stabilizing role of this form of inspection and the indispensable role of mutual inspection in any form of arms control, however limited.[46]

But, of course, mutual aerial inspection was no panacea. Aerial inspection proved capable of solving only one of four critical arms control inspection problems in the first twenty years of its use. It could monitor the installation of antiballistic missiles (ABM's), making SALT I possible; but it could not monitor underground nuclear testing, the installation of multiple independent reentry vehicles (MIRV's), camouflaged mobile missiles, or the degree of advance in antisubmarine warfare. I have no doubt that, if future arms control negotiations are to succeed, the U.S. and the U.S.S.R. will have to accept forms of mutual inspection that transcend satellite photography and provide much more flexible inspection on the ground than the "fixed control posts" of Soviet diplomacy of the 1950s.

Satellite photography was no panacea in a quite different sense. It did, of course, provide remarkable information to both sides on military production of certain kinds and order of battle; but rather full knowledge of Soviet military forces and dispositions did not guarantee an appropriate American policy. In the 1970s, for example, the United States government observed a rapid closing of the gap between U.S. and Soviet nuclear forces as well as a rapid and systematic expansion and modernization of Soviet conventional forces. The temper of the U.S. government and debates about the meaning of the Soviet effort delayed the beginnings of a serious response until the crises in Iran and Afghanistan which, in the late 1970s, played, roughly, the role of the first Sputnik twenty years earlier.

Nevertheless, mutual photographic inspection remains an indispensable and stabilizing—if not sufficient—instrument of inspection if the worst is to be avoided in a nuclear age as well as the foundation for any progress that may be achieved in arms control and arms reduction in the future. Without doubt, Eisenhower understood all this and made his proposal in Geneva in deadly earnest, launching a debate in Moscow which, along with the development of the remarkable technology of satellite photography, yielded a limited but clearly salutary result.

Turning back to the curious story of how the Open Skies proposal came to life, there is embedded in it a problem that runs forward, more or less continuously, in the U.S. government from the 1950s to the 1980s: how should a member of the White House staff, engaged on aspects of foreign policy, with direct access to the president, relate to the secretary of state? As Dulles was acutely aware, the problem was much older, involving his uncle, Secretary of State Lansing, and Colonel House during and after the First World War, as well as Hull and Stettinius in relation to Harry Hopkins and others outside the State Department a generation later. Indeed, one can trace the problem back with some legitimacy to Alexander Hamilton's challenges to Thomas Jefferson as secretary of state in the early 1790s. In the 1950s the tension centered around C. D. Jackson and, especially, Nelson Rockefeller; from 1961 forward, it centered around those who held the post of special assistant to the president for national security affairs.

A considerable literature explores this relationship, and this is not an appropriate occasion to review it. But the tension between Eisenhower and Dulles over the summit in general and, in the end, Eisenhower's need for what Rockefeller could provide do reveal, I believe, the nub of the problem: a president's role in foreign policy is, intrinsically, wider than, and in many ways distinct from, the conventional role of the secretary of state. It is not merely that the secretary of state is ultimately the president's agent; but both at home and abroad the president must be, finally, the initiator of policy; he must articulate it in political language that effectively communicates to men and women everywhere; and he must also articulate, debate, and negotiate that policy face to face with other politically responsible chiefs of government. And that policy must embrace military and economic, psychological and political factors which transcend conventional diplomacy.

It follows that the secretary of state (and his department) should, ideally, fulfill three purposes: adviser to the president in these wider foreign policy functions the president alone can fulfill; coordinator of all forms of foreign policy; and conductor of conventional diplomacy. Few secretaries of state in the post-1945 era had more reason to be confident in the primacy accorded him by his president than John Foster Dulles; but, as the testimony of Sherman Adams (pp. 39–40, above) and C. D. Jackson (pp. 48–49, above) indicates, Dulles was an anxious man: anxious about the president, anxious about the right-wing Republican senators, anxious about those engaged in economic foreign policy and arms control, and, in this case, anxious about Nelson Rockefeller and his view of what the president confronted and the initiatives he ought to take at the summit.

Given Dulles' stature and the trust Eisenhower placed in him, it should not have been difficult for him to orchestrate the various actors over the full range of foreign policy; but, somewhat like James Byrnes, he appears to have preferred to operate with a small, intimate team rather than to reach out, exploit, and manage the foreign policy establishments as a whole, with the inevitable mixed bag of strong personalities.

Eisenhower could not wholly accept the construction of a foreign policy implicit in Dulles' conception. He brought other men into play and lived as best he could with the tensions this process set up with Dulles.

As for the summit, there appears to have been, in addition to his fears of Eisenhower's "human generosity," a simple failure of imagination. From Dulles' point of view and, apparently, the view of the State Department officers concerned, the summit was regarded as an unfortunate, unavoidable, no-win venture. The systematically negative tone of the staff papers prepared for the summit in the Department of State is illustrated by the following extract from an evaluation of Soviet prospects for achieving their objectives at the conference. (The evaluations of both Soviet and U.S. prospects are given in Appendix M.)

> 1. (Moral and social equality) The Soviets will probably make considerable gains in this respect. These gains can be minimized by the President avoiding social meetings where he will be photographed with Bulganin, Kruschev [sic], etc., and by maintaining an austere countenance on occasions where photographing together is inevitable. Also, the extent of Soviet gain could be limited by public knowledge that the occasion was being used by the US to push for satellite liberation and liquidation of International Communism. Here we run into a conflict between a desire not to make the meeting into a propaganda forum and the fact that unless our position on these two topics is known, the Soviets will automatically gain very considerable advantage under this heading.

The concern reflected in this passage was by no means unjustified. It was, indeed, one of Moscow's purposes to gain increased respectability for the post-Stalin leadership at Geneva; and, once the summit was accepted, this cost was unavoidable. Churlishness would not have helped, as Eisenhower perceived. He met the Soviet delegation with his usual human warmth. The problem with Dulles' defensive assessment lay elsewhere. It led Dulles to conclude that the best strategy was narrowly to restrict Eisenhower's role on issues of substance. He did not perceive that an American president could not spend five days as the central figure in a global drama, with his three colleagues laying on the table a wide range of more or less serious substantive proposals, and confine himself to defining problems to be negotiated elsewhere. This was Rockefeller's basic, correct insight. He gambled on it; and, so far as Geneva was concerned, he won. After recounting his defeat on summit strategy (see above, pp. 49–50), Rockefeller goes on:

> So I went ahead with Lloyd Free and prepared the President's speech to make at the Geneva Conference. We got all the papers ready because I knew he would get into this bind and then he would have to come to this because after the others had made proposals and he was flatfooted he would be in an intolerable position. He would then remember this just as Harry Truman did on Point Four.
>
> It was written by somebody out of my office as Coordinator and Dean Acheson took it out of his acceptance [Truman's inaugural] speech. Then Clark Clifford, when the State Department had finished and there was nothing left in it, said, "Let's put that idea about Point Four of aid to other countries back in the speech. That has got more sex appeal than anything else." So the President put it back in and never told Acheson. And Acheson heard it when the speech was made.[47]

To what extent could Rockefeller have conducted his business in ways which would have served Eisenhower's purposes but avoided the tensions which developed with Dulles? Obviously, Rockefeller's sturdy exuberance did not make matters easier. Nor did the fact that, unlike C. D. Jackson, Rockefeller was evidently a man with further ambitions and potentialities for public service. And Eisenhower's reaching for the telephone and telling Dulles that Rockefeller had just come into his office with an interesting idea was not the most felicitous way to handle the evidently sensitive relationship between the two men. The root of the matter, however, lay in Dulles' unwillingness or inability to absorb and coordinate in a confident way the talents throughout the foreign policy establishment. As a number of analysts have observed, Dulles operated as a lawyer with Eisenhower as his client rather than the orchestrator of U.S. foreign policy as a whole. He intended to stay very close to his client and keep others from diluting or confusing his line of communication. But it is significant that he seriously considered asking for the post of special presidential assistant on foreign policy rather than secretary of state. And behind all this there may have been, as one element, a trait of personality which Gerard Smith captured in his oral history interview: "He was much happier with just three or four people, because I think basically he was a shy man. As far as I was concerned, I felt that it took me years to get really in his confidence. And after that, I was amazed how frank he was."[48]

It is also, perhaps, worth asking why Eisenhower did not take greater pains to organize the men he put to work in ways which avoided this kind of bureaucratic difficulty. Here, quite particularly, we come back to the problem which emerged in the wake of Stalin's death and which I summarized in these terms: despite the almost compulsive detail of the communications between Eisenhower and Dulles, their minds did not quite meet, as Dulles' anxieties about the summit suggest.[49] Their relationship evokes something of a Victorian novel in which two characters, closely aligned, cannot quite communicate the deepest thoughts on their minds. Eisenhower responded to Dulles' concern about potential competitors, Rockefeller and the others; but he went on using such supplementary characters. The president and his secretary of state could never quite talk the matter out and come to a definitive understanding about it.

More broadly, Eisenhower, notably after his experience in managing the collection of semiindependent allied ground, air, and naval commanders in the final stages of the Second World War in Europe, tended to take his subordinates as he found them, shrewdly assaying their strengths and weaknesses, keeping them in harness as best he could, and accepting as a fact of life that the relations among them would not always be a model of harmonious fraternity.

The underlying problems illustrated by this episode are, as noted earlier, by no means a unique result of Dulles' somewhat limited but monopolistic image of his mission; for example, the real or believed tensions between the president's assistant for national security affairs and the secretary of state became in the 1970s an endemic feature of bureaucratic life and gossip.

Behind it is a problem, not easy to solve. The problem of the 1955 summit simply illustrates one facet of a particular moment with a particular cast of characters. The problem is best illuminated by recalling what a secretary of state and a presidential adviser in foreign policy do. The post of secretary of state over the past generation is certainly the most exacting post in the government. It is loaded with inescapable overhead commitments: protracted ordeals before congressional committees; overseas trips to international conferences; an endless flow of meetings with ambassadors; White House and diplomatic dinners; state visits, with the need for fine-grained exchanges with foreign ministers; an intense series of bilateral exchanges at the annual gathering of the foreign ministers in September for the United Nations General Assembly—all this plus the need to administer a large department; to be fully informed on the state of a fissionable world; to be responsible for the daily flow of cables to every corner of the globe, of which half a dozen are liable to carry heavy freight and require that every word be weighed; and, then, the need to be prepared to render advice to the president at any hour of the day or night. A president carries, of course, the unique burden of ultimate responsibility; but, in many ways, the job of secretary of state is more onerous.

Although they have varied to a degree in each administration, the functions of the assistant for national security affairs have regularly included these five central tasks:

1. To keep the president fully informed.

2. To watch over the linkages between State, Defense, CIA, AID, the Treasury, Commerce, Agriculture, and other departments increasingly involved in foreign affairs.

3. To follow closely the development of issues within the bureaucracy so that the president knows what lies behind recommendations coming forward—notably the options rejected or washed out by bureaucratic compromise and the precise reasons why others were proposed.

4. To assist the president in his expanded personal role in diplomacy: speeches, visitors, and foreign correspondence; press contacts and trips abroad; briefings for meetings with his advisers.

5. To make sure the president's decisions are executed.

A man charged with this kind of responsibility ought to be one whose judgment the president would wish to hear, among others, before he makes a decision; and this has clearly been the case since the post, in its modern form, was created in 1961.

It is not impossible for the closely related but distinct sets of functions of the secretary of state and the special assistant to be performed in reasonable bureaucratic and human harmony. It requires, however, that the major actors understand that they are all agents of the president, who, alone among them, is an elected official; that they understand with sympathy the legitimacy of their respective chores; and that the president articulate and conduct with constancy policies which impart a sense that the lines of action being pursued in the various parts of government converge to well-understood purposes. But, in the end, the coherence and collegiality of the team managing foreign affairs are determined by the personalities of those whom the president chooses and by his capacity, as a leader, to keep them effectively in harness. Truman's administration was one thing when Byrnes was secretary of state, quite another when Marshall and Acheson held the post; it operated in a tense and acrimonious way with Louis Johnson as secretary of defense, as a model of inner harmony with Robert Lovett presiding at the Pentagon.

The Eisenhower first term was not marked, as post-1945 administrations go, by particularly acute inner tensions in the conduct of its foreign policy. In part, this was the case because, relatively speaking, the period from Stalin's death in March 1953 to the nationalization of the Suez Canal in July 1956 was an interval of pause and calm in the Cold War. It was also the result of Eisenhower's political popularity and working style, which fitted well such a relatively quiet time. Nevertheless, the story of the 1955 summit and Open Skies suggests that State Department–White House relations were rather awkward despite the formidable machinery of inter-departmental staff work and cooperation which Eisenhower created in 1953.

Open Skies also illustrates a narrower endemic problem in the American bureaucracy which is worth noting because Dulles was conscious of it. It will be recalled that in his complaint to Eisenhower about Rockefeller on August 5, 1955, Dulles said, in his memorandum of conversation (p. 42, above): "I recognized that the regular departments were often so tied to daily routines that they did not have time or resourcefulness in dealing with new ideas." In his oral history interview William Macomber addressed himself at some length to Dulles' view of this problem:

> He [Dulles] worried a great deal about the lack of ideas in the Department. I remember one time, some people came running in. There was an international meeting coming up, and the task force had been set up in the White House to prepare for this meeting. And, a number of people came in all upset. "This is the State Department's business. What are these task forces for?" So, of course, they were saying, "Mr. Dulles, you have to call the President and put a stop to this." So he did.
> But then when it was called off, and it was clear this was

the State Department's business—other people's views would be welcome, but any papers were going to be prepared in the State Department; they were in charge of it—and when all that was reestablished, he put the phone back down, and he turned to the group in the room, and he said, "Look, fellows. Okay. It's back in your jurisdiction. But let me say this to you. The State Department is not going to stay in control of foreign policy just because its title is the State Department. It's only going to stay in control of the foreign policy of this country—and control in the sense of being the dominant Department—if it has the ideas." He said, "I don't get the impression that we're coming up with the ideas. And if we don't, this Department is not going to stay on top of things."

Then later, returning to that subject, he said to me, "How can we break this? What can we do to get more original thinking coming to me? Honestly, can you think of an original idea that's come out of the Department since I've been Secretary of State—a really, truly original idea?"

And I said, "Why, certainly, a number of ideas."

He said, "Well, name one."

And, by golly, I couldn't think of a genuinely original idea.

"Well," Mr. Dulles said, "I can name one that came forward in recent time, and that's the 'open skies' proposal. That's an original idea. I don't know where it came from, but I don't think it came from the State Department. It may have come from the meeting in Quantico. It may have come from a number of places, but it didn't come from here. Now, we've got to get more original thinking in this building. It's tough enough to keep control of foreign policy—to keep it from getting fragmented—but that's really going to go on, if the Department of State thinks it's just going to stay in control because of organizational charts—it's not so. How can we stimulate some original thinking?"

And we talked about it.

He finally said, "You know, I think what's happening is that the young fellows have some pretty original ideas, but the Assistant Secretary level is probably what's holding it back. The Assistant Secretary level is much more experienced, and they know all the reasons why these things won't work, and so they tend to listen, but that's where it stops. It doesn't come on up to me, because they see flaws in it, and so I don't get exposed to any of it." He said, "I think I'm going to ask [and he did ask at the next staff meeting] that the Assistant Secretaries of State encourage these ideas and pass them on to me, even though in their original form they probably are unworkable. They're perfectly free to make their comments about why they're unworkable. But if they are original, there should be an effort to get them up to me. Because maybe even if they are unacceptable in the form that they're first presented, they may stimulate a thought that will be original and can be done a different way."

I remember that was tried. I don't recall any great idea that came out of that, but the point I'm making is that he was fretting about the lack of original thinking.[50]

As one who worked in the State Department, in 1945–1946 and 1961–1966, and had occasion to observe it closely for much longer periods, I understand with some sympathy the problem Dulles posed. At any moment of time, the members of that department are engaged in trying to carry out existing policy. That policy is set by the president, translated into detailed instructions by the secretary of state, and then incorporated into a flow of cables and other communications geared to events as they unfold from day to day. This is hard, absorbing work; and minimum order requires that all hands, in Washington and abroad, adhere with precision to the lines of existing policy.

In the usual case, excepting a change of administrations, policy is sharply altered only when a crisis arises which reveals existing policies are no longer viable. The normal conduct of U.S. foreign policy illustrates admirably Jean Monnet's dictum: "Men only accept change in the face of necessity; and they see that necessity only when confronted by crisis." Decisions taken during the crisis tend to move up in hierarchy and over to the White House, where the secretary of state and a few senior officials from the State Department are involved. As the crisis subsides and the dust settles, new policies emerge, are translated into working guidelines, transmitted around the world, and the bureaucracy settles down again to orderly operations on a new course.

Change is inherently painful and disruptive in a bureaucracy. It takes ingenuity and stubborn dedication to keep the machine turning over with reasonable efficiency on a given course. There is not much time for those operating the machine to devote to possible new courses of action, and new ideas generally meet a good deal of resistance. And they should, because to be effective they must meet the test of viability in a world full of sharp-edged problems that cannot be exorcised by rhetoric or goodwill. As Dulles told Macomber, the State Department traditionally excels in criticizing a new proposal and isolating the problems it will confront if set in motion.

Nevertheless, a president usually realizes more vividly than any other officer in the government that new ideas and courses of action are essential to cope with a fast-changing world and his rather special place within it. Inside the State Department a Policy Planning Council exists to generate new policy initiatives. And strong, creative men and women in other parts of the State Department have generated ideas which enriched U.S. foreign policy. In the 1950s the Policy Planning Staff, quite particularly, made significant contributions to both foreign aid policy and arms control. But in 1955, on the summit in general and Open Skies in particular, the Policy Planning Staff did not come actively into play—perhaps because Dulles' basic view of the summit was rather negative and apprehensive.

Ultimately, however, the problem of developing new ideas in the Washington bureaucracy is not a matter of formal organization. It depends on the president creating an atmosphere in which every public servant knows that new ideas are welcome and needed. Franklin Roosevelt succeeded in generating that sense of the value attached to invention and innovation in his first term, and it pervaded Washington in the administrations of Kennedy and Johnson. In such a setting, the problem posed by the kind of tension which emerged between Dulles and Rockefeller should be handled by what might be called the Rusk Rule. When I served Secretary of State Rusk as chairman of the Policy Planning Council, Kennedy and then Johnson instructed me to send over to them directly any ideas I thought might be useful. Rusk approved the arrangement with the simple proviso that I send him a copy of anything transmitted directly to the White House. When, in 1966, I moved into the post of special assistant to the president for national security affairs, Johnson indicated he wished me to continue to propose new foreign policy initiatives. Rusk observed that new ideas were generally in short supply and that a president should look everywhere for them; he merely asked for copies of anything of this kind which I generated so that when the president requested his view he would have had the opportunity to formulate it. Rusk's request was honored, and there was no difficulty over the matter.

In 1955 there is no evidence that Rockefeller ever failed to inform Dulles of any proposal he laid before the president, and life in Washington would have been somewhat simpler if Dulles had confined his anxieties within the Rusk Rule.

The final question posed by the story of Open Skies is a good deal larger than these rather narrow bureaucratic issues—and more problematical. The question is whether Eisenhower, by failing to react vigorously to the clear evidence of Soviet ambitious intentions in 1955 and, in particular, failing to accept Rockefeller's proposals incorporated in Quantico Panel II, lost an opportunity to prevent the tense and dangerous confrontations that wracked the world from the Suez crisis of 1956 to the Cuba missile crisis of 1962.

As indicated earlier, the Soviet offensive over which Khrushchev assumed unambiguous command from June 1957 was based on two concepts germinating from the early 1950s forward: (1) nuclear blackmail, that is, the use of the threat represented by nuclear-armed missiles to advance Soviet diplomatic and political authority, and (2) the exploitation to Soviet advantage of the strands of assertive, anti-Western nationalism endemic in Latin America, Africa, the Middle East, and Asia by programs of military, economic, and political assistance. In this process, Khrushchev's hand was strengthened by Castro's commitment to Communism, formalized in the summer of 1958, and by the stubborn, large ambitions of the Communist government in Hanoi. The offensive was conducted against a backdrop of increasingly acute crisis between the Soviet Union and the People's Republic of China, starting early in 1958 and within the limit of avoiding war with the United States.

In this setting the launching of the first Sputnik in October 1957 played a dual role and was, from Khrushchev's point of view, something of a two-edged sword. First, in all its psychological and political ramifications it imparted a sense of historic opportunity and confidence to Communist leaders throughout the world. As in the 1970s, they came to believe the "correlation of forces" had yielded "new power realities" which they had a duty to exploit and the West to accept. Second, it generated pressure on Khrushchev from the Chinese and others to achieve concrete results.

Thus, the quite unnecessary Soviet leadership in launching a space satellite was costly—initially to the United States and, over time, to the Soviet Union. It heightened the case in Moscow for the campaign to deceive the world about the Soviet ICBM capability, alarmed U.S. allies about the vulnerability of the U.S. strategic deterrent, and heightened the blackmail possibilities in Europe of the MRBM's and IRBM's. In the Communist world it helped trigger a phase of expansionist enterprise. In the developing regions it provided a backdrop for Soviet efforts to extend power and influence in Asia, the Middle East, Africa, and Latin America. For the Soviet Union, the train of events also set in motion by the launching of the first Sputnik ended with the severe setback of the Cuba missile crisis.[51]

An increase in the U.S. military budget in 1956 and other actions along the lines suggested in Quantico II might have substantially mitigated the reaction to the launching of the first Sputnik in both the Communist and the non-Communist worlds. As things happened, the United States was put in a reactive, defensive posture. If Eisenhower had gone to the country in the wake of the disappointing events of 1955, explained that the Soviet Union was in the process of narrowing the military gap, and proposed measures to avoid that outcome, the setting in which Sputnik was launched would have been considerably different. On a matter of this kind, I would guess he would have commanded strong bipartisan support within the Congress and outside.

It is a much more complex matter to assess the extent to which the launching in 1956 of an enlarged program of assistance to the developing regions would have mitigated the crises faced by the United States in the later 1950s. A decision by the United States and the West to go ahead with the building of the Aswân Dam might, conceivably, have kept Nasser on a more even, less inflammatory course; an Alliance for Progress launched in 1956 might have presented Castro with less attractive prospects than appeared open to him as a Communist operative in 1958. It is less clear that such policies would have affected greatly the course of events in the Congo and Hanoi's decision to resume in 1958 its efforts to take over South Vietnam.

The latter decision flowed from two strands at work in the Moscow conference of November 1957: (1) the agreement among Communist leaders that the moment was propitious for efforts to expand Communist power and (2) the competition between Moscow and Peking for Hanoi's allegiance, which the North Vietnamese exploited to receive support from both for the resumed pursuit of its ambitions in Indochina.[52] Only a U.S. military and space policy and posture which avoided the Moscow meeting and the phase of Communist post-Sputnik euphoria in 1957–1958 might have postponed or deflected that decision. The prior U.S. launching of an enlarged program of development assistance might have played an ancillary role in that damping process, but it was clearly not a central factor.

This kind of counterfactual exercise is of extremely limited utility, but it relates to a larger fact and a larger question. The fact is that in the late 1950s and early 1960s American policy was pushed piecemeal by the course of events and the reflections on them of both American leaders and public opinion to move in the directions Quantico Panel II counseled in 1955, notably, an enlarged military establishment and enlarged programs of development assistance, including nations not allied to the United States. And, before a reasonable but transient equilibrium in U.S.-Soviet relations was reestablished in the wake of the Cuba missile crisis, the world had transited a good many rather unpleasant and even dangerous crises. To some extent impossible to measure, these might have been avoided or mitigated if the U.S. response to Soviet military and space policy had been more forehanded and its approach to the developing regions more imaginative. At both Quantico I and Quantico II such a response was urged on the U.S. government, and the members of those panels were by no means unique in their perceptions.

The question is: why was Eisenhower so slow to respond? So far as military policy is concerned, there was a convergence in his mind of an authentic sense that the U.S. nuclear strategic position was adequate and a passionate conviction that the constraint of federal expenditures was an exceedingly high, if not overriding, criterion for public policy. In his own phrase, he aimed "to conduct a revolution" to reverse the rising trend in the federal budget;[53] and, as the economy "sputtered" in his second term, and the budget surpluses of

1956–1957 gave way to deficits in 1958–1959, Eisenhower's concern became almost obsessional. He was left in the position of counseling his successor on January 19, 1961, that he might well have to put U.S. forces into Laos but leaving to him a military establishment with inadequate mobility and the bulk of the conventional forces in strategic reserve earmarked for a NATO shadowed by Khrushchev's ultimatum on Berlin.

On space, Eisenhower, like most of his colleagues, simply suffered failure of imagination on the question of primacy in launching an earth satellite; and he regarded the whole space program—notably, the notion of manned flight to the moon —as something the United States could simply not afford.

On economic development assistance, he understood its importance in U.S. foreign policy from 1954, if not earlier, but was distinctly ambivalent in leading the nation to accept an enlarged foreign aid effort. (The evolution of U.S. foreign aid policy in the 1950s will be dealt with at length in the forthcoming fifth book in this series.) In 1958, for example, he encouraged a massive effort by a bipartisan citizens' committee, headed by Eric Johnston, to rally public support for the program he had put before the Congress. I served on Johnston's committee. In February it sponsored a remarkable gathering in Washington, addressed by, among others, Eisenhower and Nixon, Truman and Acheson, Stevenson and Allen Dulles, Fulton J. Sheen and James Killian. Eisenhower received his ardent lobbyists in his office on April 8, 1958. Expecting a statement of encouragement and an injunction to carry on the good fight, most of us were shaken to hear a troubled and wistful monologue about the overriding need to balance the budget, closing with the rhetorical question: "Where are we going to get the money from?"

In the end, then, Eisenhower's rejection of Rockefeller's advice at the close of 1955 was an authentic expression of the budgetary policy of his administration, as was the phalanx of opposition Rockefeller confronted in the Treasury, the Department of Defense, and the Bureau of the Budget.

As in each of the three earlier books in this series, the story of Open Skies and all that lay behind it comes to rest in part, then, on the matter of timing. In the six years which followed the completion of Quantico Panel reports I and II, the United States had, by and large, done the things those reports had counseled if Soviet behavior at the summit and elsewhere indicated that Moscow's intentions were not authentically pacific. The U.S. acted not because those reports were judged, at last, to be wise, for few read them. The U.S. acted because a sequence of events gradually persuaded the leaders in American political life that a more vigorous military policy and a policy addressed directly to the tasks of growth and social progress in the developing regions were in the U.S. interest. U.S. actions were taken piecemeal and with important delays. Meanwhile, Soviet policy pursued doggedly the openings history and the weaknesses in U.S. policy appeared to afford.

The story thus illustrates reasons for the roughly cyclical character of U.S.-Soviet relations over the past four decades. The United States and the Soviet Union are by no means the only relevant actors on the world stage; and, with the passage of time, the stage has been progressively crowding up. But the policy of each of the two superpowers has been and continues to be addressed to problems and situations where the role of each has been determined, to a significant degree, by the image of the other. Specifically, the Soviet Union, the less powerful but highly ambitious partner in the game, has systematically assessed the openings offered by the course of history and U.S. policy and has moved to exploit them when their exploitation did not appear to involve a serious risk of war with the United States. Thus occurred Stalin's policy toward Europe in 1945–1949 and his adventure of 1950–1953 with Mao and Kim in Korea; Khrushchev's post-Sputnik offensive of 1958–1962; and Brezhnev's adventures in Africa, the Caribbean, the Middle East, and Southeast Asia of the 1970s. In each case the U.S. has reacted, but with a lag in a rapidly deteriorating situation: in 1947–1950 with the Marshall Plan and NATO in Europe and by fighting a war in Korea; by sealing off the intrusions in the Caribbean, Africa, and Southeast Asia as well as dealing with the Berlin ultimatum in 1961–1962; and by moving in 1979–1980 to protect the flow of oil from the Persian Gulf in the wake of the Soviet incursion into Afghanistan, as well as by reaffirming the validity of the Southeast Asia Treaty with respect to Thailand. In all three cases, increases in the U.S. military budget were required to cope with the crises which resulted from the openings U.S. policy appeared to present to the Soviet Union and the sluggishness of the American response to the enterprises Moscow launched on the basis of its perceptions of opportunity. In all three cases, there were those who warned of the dangers for the United States implicit in the situation as it must appear in Moscow and urged an anticipatory sealing off of the danger. But the U.S. political process appeared incapable of anticipatory action and moved only in the face of palpable crisis, while the Soviet political process appeared incapable of anticipating what the U.S. response to its initiatives was, in the end, likely to be or judged that, on balance, it would emerge from the delayed American response with a net advantage.

What we have here is a curious parallel to the economist's case of duopoly: a market with only two competitive producers where the action of each plays back on the behavior of the other and the outcome can only be cutthroat competition *à outrance*, yielding a clean-cut victory for one or a market-sharing deal. The facts of life in a nuclear age have thus far fended off the monopolistic outcome, setting limits on the competitive struggle; but the terms for stable and mutually acceptable rules of behavior have not been found. The dreary lagged cycle first set in motion in the wake of the

Second World War has continued precariously through its third round, with its two major protagonists progressively weakened by strains within their economies and the diffusion of power on the world scene in all except its nuclear dimension. Aside from Soviet ambitions, the engine driving the cycle forward has been the incapacity of the American political process to sustain a military and foreign policy course that is, at once, both steady and anticipatory. The story of the 1955 summit and its aftermath illuminates the mechanism of that recurrent American failure.

Thus, Eisenhower did not succeed in 1955–1956 any better than did Truman in 1945–1946 or Ford and Carter in the mid 1970s in heading off a degenerative process requiring a later, rather convulsive American response. But he did approach foreign policy in his time with a kind of statesman's view which he felt Khrushchev lacked (see above, p. 9). He was acutely aware of the dangers to all mankind in a nuclear age; he authentically believed the only rational course for the United States and the Soviet Union was arms control; and Open Skies represented "a tiny gate in the disarmament fence" he struggled to open.

He also understood that the contest between the United States and the Soviet Union in the developing regions was likely to prove no less frustrating than the U.S.-Soviet arms race. And he was capable of bringing the two themes together as he did in an address before the special emergency session of the U.N. General Assembly on August 13, 1958:

> As I look out on this Assembly, with many of you representing new nations, one thought above all impresses me. The world that is being remade on our planet is going to be a world of many mature nations. As one after another of these nations moves through the difficult transition to modernization and learns the methods of growth, from this travail new levels of prosperity and productivity will emerge. This world of individual nations is not going to be con-

trolled by any one power or group of powers. It is not going to be committed to any one ideology. Please believe me when I say that the dream of world domination by any one power or of world conformity is an impossible dream. The nature of today's weapons, the nature of modern communications, and the widening circle of new nations make it plain that we must, in the end, be a world community of open societies. And the concept of the open society is the key to a system of arms control we can all trust.[54]

Appendix A

Documents Bearing on the 6:00 P.M. July 20, 1955, Meeting

[*Note:* This appendix contains Goodpaster's and Dillon Anderson's accounts of the critical meeting on the evening of July 20; a supplementary memorandum of Goodpaster's indicating belated briefing of officials in Washington; and Stassen's proposal for a presidential statement (before Open Skies was accepted), considered at the evening meeting of July 20. (From the Dwight D. Eisenhower Papers, Ann Whitman Files, International Meetings Series, box 1, "Geneva Conference, July 18–23, 1955" folder 3, Dwight D. Eisenhower Library.)]

July 25, 1955

MEMORANDUM FOR RECORD:
Meeting at the President's Villa, 6 PM, 20 July 1955
Present: The President
            Secretary Dulles
            Mr. Dillon Anderson
            General Gruenther
            Governor Stassen
            Admiral Radford
            Mr. Rockefeller
            Deputy Secretary Anderson
            Colonel Goodpaster
    Governor Stassen handed out a draft statement on disarmament, of which the most striking idea was that of indicating willingness to agree to permit overflights of the U.S. and the USSR for aerial pho-

tography as a device for inspection.* Mr. Robert Anderson indicated that the furnishing of lists of military installations should be coupled with that.

The President thought the great value of an inspection system placed in actual operations would be to begin to enable confidence to be developed on the part of the various nations as to just what military forces and installations existed in the other countries.

Secretary Dulles asked whether this proposal would pertain just to the United States and USSR or whether it would be applied to the NATO area, in line with the interest of the British. General Gruenther brought out that there are some special secure areas within Western Europe—some special geographical arrangements for putting the scheme into effect might therefore have to be developed. Governor Stassen commented on this scheme, as well as on schemes which have a zonal basis. He said that it would tend to fix the "iron curtain" more firmly. The President thought the effect would be just the opposite, if it were measured from the present—since there would be inspection teams going into areas now behind the iron curtain. Mr. Stassen also pointed out that inspection might let the USSR obtain information on our own advanced technology and insist on looking at our nuclear weapons, etc. in detail.

Mr. Robert Anderson felt that a scheme with the three principal elements—1) photography; 2) application to the US and USSR; 3) concurrent ground inspection—would provide a useful beginning, and would not extend so far as to permit detailed inspection of new technological developments. The President asked if it would not be better to suggest that all four countries permit inspection of this type. Mr. Dulles said that if this proposal were made, we would be under some obligation to discuss it with our allies before advancing it. Mr. Anderson recalled his point of requiring that lists of military installations be furnished, but said that inspection would not be limited simply to the sites named in the list. General Gruenther asked whether there would be ground inspection, and Mr. Robert

[*The text of Stassen's memorandum does not, in fact, include the concept of mutual aerial inspection. It merely asserts U.S. willingness to proceed in the study and testing of a reliable system of inspections and reporting. See below, p. 110.]

Anderson said there would be but not everything would be available for examination. Admiral Radford said that we would agree to a proposal of this kind, and Governor Stassen repeated that advanced technology should be excluded from the items to be inspected. General Gruenther said he felt that the overflight proposal had a great deal to recommend it. Mr. Stassen said this proposal could constitute a splendid opening step in the move toward disarmament. Mr. Dulles thought that from the standpoints both of drama and substance the proposal was very promising and should have a very great effect. He added, however, that if word got out in advance about this idea, much of the impact would be lost.

There was extended discussion as to the tactics to be used, resulting in agreement that it would be best for the President to make a broad and basic opening statement giving his over-all views in the matter, and then on the "second round" put forward the proposal for overflights as a specific, more or less spontaneous, suggestion.

A. J. Goodpaster
Colonel, CE, US Army

July 21, 1955

MEMORANDUM FOR THE RECORD:

At a meeting at 6:00 P.M. on Wednesday, July 20, 1955, in the President's Villa at Geneva, the following attended:

The President
The Secretary of State
Mr. Livingston Merchant,
   Assistant Secretary of State
   for European Affairs
General Alfred M. Gruenther,
   Supreme Allied Commander in Europe
Admiral Arthur W. Radford,
   Chairman, Joint Chiefs of Staff
Mr. Robert B. Anderson,
   Deputy Secretary of Defense
Mr. Harold E. Stassen,
   Special Assistant to the President on Disarmament

Mr. Nelson A. Rockefeller,
  Special Assistant to the President
Mr. Dillon Anderson,
  Special Assistant to the President
  for National Security Affairs
Colonel Andrew J. Goodpaster,
  White House Staff Secretary

Governor Stassen handed to the President and read a "Draft of Statement of President Eisenhower on the Subject of Disarmament." A copy of that instrument is attached to the original of this memorandum.

The President expressed himself as being entirely in agreement with the principles enunciated in the paper, particularly with reference to the importance of an effective inspection system in connection with any kind of disarmament agreement. In the discussion which followed, those in attendance proceeded to consider the several possible areas and methods of inspection as a part of steps that might be taken to test the efficacy and practicality of disarmament programs.

The President reported briefly on his discussion at breakfast with the British Prime Minister and the Foreign Secretary, and the fact that the British were in accord with our view as to the importance of effective inspection as a part of any kind of disarmament program; also the desirability of exploring in this Conference the possibilities of progress in this direction.

There was a discussion of the possibility of armaments limitation in the context of a divided Germany; of limited armaments in zones in Germany in each side of a neutral zone; and of some kind of limitation of forces in NATO nations and in the nations participating in the Warsaw Agreement. (There was no mention of the matter discussed with the British as to the possibility of limitation of armaments and inspection by all participants in the Warsaw Treaty except Russia on the east, and all participants in NATO on the west except the United Kingdom and the United States.)

General Gruenther pointed out that there was a sort of inspection going on now, in the form of the so-called Potsdam teams—namely, representatives of the East were permitted to travel in West Germany, and a team from the West had not been denied access to any installations in East Germany. General Gruenther apparently seemed to feel that this was a program that was working.

When it was mentioned that this system might be extended, General Gruenther pointed out that from our standpoint we would have to be very particular about its going into effect, inasmuch as we had some very sensitive installations in adjacent areas—installations which had been so apparent from the heavy security surrounding them that a visiting Congressman recently had no difficulty in recognizing the location of these sensitive installations.

The President mentioned the fact that at breakfast with the British he had indicated to them his belief that a plan for mutual overflights in the East and West, to include Russia and the United States, would not be unacceptable to him. (This subject likewise is dealt with on page 4 of the Stassen memorandum.)

There was general agreement at the meeting that in the plenary session of Thursday afternoon the President could appropriately suggest consideration of a plan to permit such overflights and photographs if the Russians would do likewise. The President pointed out that in his opinion, the Russians already had the means of knowing the location of virtually all our installations, and that mutual agreements for such overflights would undoubtedly benefit us more than the Russians because we knew very little about their installations.

The question then arose as to whether it would be entirely appropriate for this idea to be advanced at the meeting Thursday afternoon without some advice to the British and French beforehand. It was decided that there would be no such disclosure or tripartite discussion of the plan, in view of the likelihood that the impact of it would be lost through a leak. It was likewise agreed that the President would not include it in his opening statement on disarmament, but would mention it, in more or less extemporaneous fashion, on the "second round" . . .

DILLON ANDERSON
Special Assistant
to the President

MEMORANDUM FOR THE RECORD:
At the close of the discussion at 6 PM on 20 July separately reported
by Dillon Anderson, Deputy Secretary Anderson suggested that Secretary Hoover might inform Senator [Walter] George, Congressman
[James P.] Richards and one or two others of the proposal on inspection which the President has in mind to make. They would not be
caught by surprise as a result. The President suggested to Secretary
Dulles that he might do this at once, stressing the need for secrecy,
and indicating that he hoped Congressional leaders would be able
to express quick support of the idea.

(This was done by Secretary Dulles' cable of early 21 July.)

A. J. Goodpaster
Colonel, CE, US Army

STASSEN DRAFT OF
STATEMENT OF PRESIDENT EISENHOWER ON THE
SUBJECT OF DISARMAMENT
Considered at meeting on evening of July 20, 1955

Mr. Chairman, Gentlemen:
Disarmament is one of the most important subjects on our
agenda. It is also extremely difficult. In recent years the scientists
have discovered methods of making weapons many, many times
more destructive of opposing armed forces—but also of homes,
and industries and lives—than ever known or even imagined before. These same scientific discoveries have made more complex
the problems of limitation and control and reduction of armament.
After our victory as Allies in World War II, my country rapidly
disarmed. Within a few years our armament was at a very low level.
Then events occurred beyond our borders which caused us to
realize that we had disarmed too much. For our own security and to
safeguard peace we needed greater strength. Therefore we proceeded to rearm and to associate with others in a partnership for
peace and for mutual security.

The American people are determined to maintain and if necessary increase this armed strength for as long a period as is necessary to safeguard peace and to maintain our security.

But we know that a mutually dependable system for less armament on the part of all nations would be a better way to safeguard peace and to maintain our security.

It would ease the fears of war in the anxious hearts of people everywhere. It would lighten the burdens upon the backs of the people. It would make it possible for every nation, great and small, developed and less developed, to advance the standards of living of its people, to attain better food, and clothing, and shelter, more of education and larger enjoyment of life.

Therefore the United States government is prepared to enter into a sound and reliable agreement making possible the reduction of armament. I have directed that an intensive and thorough study of this subject be made. From these studies, which are continuing, a very important principle is emerging to which I referred in my opening statement on Monday.

No sound and reliable agreement can be made unless it is completely covered by an inspection and reporting system adequate to support every portion of the agreement.

The lessons of history teach us that disarmament agreements without adequate reciprocal inspection increase the dangers of war and do not brighten the prospects of peace.

Thus it is my view that the priority attention of our combined study of disarmament should be upon the subject of inspection and reporting.

How effective an inspection system can be designed which would be mutually and reciprocally acceptable within our countries and the other nations of the world? How would such a system operate? What could it accomplish?

Is certainty against surprise aggression attainable by inspection? Could violations be discovered promptly and effectively counteracted?

We have not as yet been able to discover any scientific or other inspection method which would make certain of the elimination of nuclear weapons. So far as we are aware no other nation has made such a discovery. Our study of this problem is continuing. We have not as yet been able to discover any accounting or other inspection method of being certain of the true budgetary facts of total expenditures for armament. Our study of this problem is continuing. We by no means exclude the possibility of finding useful checks in these fields.

As you can see from these statements, it is our impression that many past proposals of disarmament are more sweeping than can be insured by effective inspection.*

From my statements I believe you will anticipate my suggestion. It is that we instruct our representatives in the U N Subcommittee on Disarmament in discharge of their mandate from the United Nations to give priority effort to the study of inspection and reporting. Such a study could well include a step by step testing of inspection and reporting methods.

The United States is ready to proceed in the study and testing of a reliable system of inspections and reporting, and when that system is proved, then to reduce armaments with all others to the extent that the system will provide assured results.

The successful working out of such a system would do much to develop the mutual confidence which will open wide the avenues of progress for all our peoples.

The quest for peace is the statesman's most exacting duty. Security of the nation entrusted to his care is his greatest responsibility. Practical progress to lasting peace is his fondest hope. Yet in pursuit of his hope he must not betray the trust placed in him as guardian of the people's security. A sound peace—with security, justice, wellbeing, and freedom for the people of the world—*can* be achieved, but only by patiently and thoughtfully following a hard and sure and tested road.

[*At this point Eisenhower introduced the Open Skies proposal in his statement of July 21. See above, pp. 6–7.]

Appendix B

Notes on the Eisenhower-Eden Meeting,
Breakfast, July 20, 1955

[*Note:* Appendix B includes Ann Whitman's report and transcript of Dillon Anderson's notes on the meeting between Eisenhower and Eden early on July 20. Only the discussion of disarmament is included here. A brief passage (noted by X's) has not yet been declassified. (From the Dwight D. Eisenhower Papers, Ann Whitman Files, International Meetings Series, box 1, "Geneva Conference, July 18–23, 1955" folder 3, Dwight D. Eisenhower Library.)]

Wednesday, July 20.

This morning the President had early breakfast with Sir Anthony Eden, Secretary Dulles and Harold Macmillan, and Dillon Anderson. Dillon Anderson dictated the following memorandum of conversation. (He later made some revisions, which I do not have.)

"Then came the subject of disarmament. The President indicated that Governor Stassen had been giving very intensive thought to this subject; that Governor Stassen would be in Geneva today, and stated that he and Mr. Dulles and Governor Stassen had all reached the conclusion that the very heart of any such arrangement lay in the efficacy of the inspections systems that would be parts of it. X X X X It was agreed that the best way to counter this was to point out the incompleteness of the inspection system that the Russians had proposed and cited the fact that in Korea such a system had failed to work. It was apparently agreed between those at breakfast that we should in this meeting propose in the area of a limited or test inspection plan or system in connection with the forces in opposition to each other in

Europe. There was some further discussion of the position of Germany in this connection and the possibility of a demilitarized zone with forces on each side limited by agreement and subject to effective inspection. The President suggested that such an inspection system might in the first instance be one that would exclude the Soviet Union, but include East Germany and the satellite countries, the Eastern bloc being permitted to inspect the Western countries except the United Kingdom and the United States. The President said he would be agreeable to some plan including all of our installations, since without an Iron Curtain on our side the Russians know exactly where the installations are and what they are anyway. He said he would even be willing to go further and agree to over-flights and he did not feel there would be anything lost to us in such a connection. Mr. Dulles mentioned the possibility of this being difficult in connection with war games and similar exercises. The President said he would just as soon let them witness these. He stressed the fact that the Russians have means already of knowing all the facts about our military installations and their locations, and cited the fact that in the Smyth report the complete map and plot of Hanford was illustrated—a perfect bomber's map.

"After the breakfast was over, Secretary Dulles stepped out of the room for a moment. The President and Eden stood and talked, and Eden seemed to me to press him for an agreement that the United States would agree in this conference to the adoption of some specific arrangement of an arms limitation and inspection plan participated in between the Eastern and Western powers and applicable to Europe. This seemed to me to be an extension of the degree of commitment which had been contemplated before we came to Geneva; in other words, the initial policy seemed to be that we had agreed to the exploration by the Ministers of specific plans, but here there seems to be an agreement that the Heads of State would actually approve some particular features of such a plan."

Appendix C

Soviet Inspection Proposals of May 10, 1955, and the Initial U.S. Reaction

[*Note:* These Soviet proposals for fixed international inspection posts and the initial guarded U.S. response were included in a large set of disarmament proposals, although the position taken on control was clearly the most important new feature. (From the Department of State *Bulletin* 32, no. 831, May 30, 1955, pp. 900–905.)]

CONCERNING INTERNATIONAL CONTROL OVER THE REDUCTION OF ARMAMENTS AND THE PROHIBITION OF ATOMIC WEAPONS

The General Assembly.

Recognizing the great importance and the necessity of instituting effective international control over the fulfillment by States of their obligations under the convention on the reduction of armaments and armed forces and the prohibition of atomic and hydrogen weapons,

Notes that the requisite conditions for the institution of a control system which would enjoy the confidence of all States and would fully meet the requirements of international security do not at present exist.

It is impossible to disregard the fact that there exists at present considerable international tension and mistrust in relations between States. It is this that accounts for the fact that, in the conditions of mistrust among States which have come into being, barriers of every sort are being erected even in regard to the interchange of industrial, agricultural, scientific, cultural and other delegations.

Such a situation renders difficult the attainment of agreement providing for States to grant access to those undertakings, particularly those engaged in military production, to foreign control officials who might carry out the inspection of such undertakings.

In the present circumstances, in which many States are displaying legitimate anxiety for their security, it can hardly be expected that they should trustingly provide other States with facilities for access to industrial and other resources of theirs which are vital to their security.

In so far as the necessary trust does not at the present time exist between States, a situation may arise in which the adoption of decisions on international control will in reality be reduced to a mere formality which does not achieve the objective. Such a possibility is the most inadmissible in that very great fears exist among peaceloving peoples, in present conditions, in connexion with the existence of atomic and hydrogen weapons, in regard to which the institution of international control is particularly difficult.

This danger is inherent in the very nature of atomic production. It is well known that the production of atomic energy for peaceful purposes can be used for the accumulation of stocks of explosive atomic materials, and for their accumulation in constantly increasing quantities. This means that States having establishments for the production of atomic energy can accumulate, in contravention of the relevant agreements, large quantities of explosive materials for the production of atomic weapons. The danger of this state of affairs is particularly clear in view of the fact that where the requisite quantities of explosive atomic materials exist production of actual atomic and hydrogen bombs is technically perfectly feasible and can be effected on a large scale.

Thus, even given the existence of a formal agreement on international control, opportunities, which cannot be covered by the international control system, exist for evading such control and for organizing the clandestine manufacture of atomic and hydrogen weapons. In these circumstances, the security of the States signatories to the international convention cannot be guaranteed, since it would be open to a potential aggressor to accumulate stocks of atomic and hydrogen weapons for a surprise attack on peaceloving States.

Until an atmosphere of confidence has been created in relations between States, any agreement on the institution of international control can only serve to lull the vigilance of the peoples. It will create a false sense of security despite the actual existence of the threat of the production of atomic and hydrogen weapons and consequently also of the threat of surprise attack and the unleashing of an atomic war with all its appalling consequences for the peoples.

It must also be borne in mind that preparations for a new war, the danger of which has been vastly increased by the development of atomic and hydrogen weapons, inevitably necessitate the concentration of large military formations at certain points together with large quantities of conventional armaments—aircraft, artillery, tanks, warships and so forth. The concentration and movement of large formations of land, sea and air forces cannot be effected except through important communication centres, ports and airfields. Under conditions of modern military technique, the importance of such points in the preparation of an aggressive war has not diminished, but is on the contrary increasing.

In addition to atomic and hydrogen weapons, for all their destructive capacity, armies of many millions and great quantities of conventional armaments, which are of decisive importance to the outcome of any major war, would inevitably be involved in military operations in the onset of the outbreak of war.

All this must be taken into account in dealing with the problem of instituting international control over the fulfillment by States of their obligations under the convention on the reduction of armaments and the prohibition of atomic weapons.

The problem of instituting international control and of the rights and powers of the international control organ must therefore be considered in close connexion with the execution of the above-mentioned measures for the relaxation of international tension, the strengthening of trust between States and the carrying out of other measures relating to the reduction of armaments and the prohibition of atomic weapons.

In view of the foregoing,

The General Assembly institutes an international control organ having the following rights and powers:

116

1. *During the first stage* of execution of the measures for the reduction of armaments and the prohibition of atomic weapons,

    (a) in order to prevent a surprise attack by one State upon another, the international control organ shall establish on the territory of all the States concerned, on a basis of reciprocity, control posts at large ports, at railway junctions, on main motor highways and in aerodromes. The function of these posts shall be to ensure that no dangerous concentration of military land forces or of air or naval forces takes place.

    (b) the international control organ shall have the right to require from States any necessary information on the execution of measures for the reduction of armaments and armed forces.

    (c) the control organ shall have unimpeded access to records relating to the budgetary appropriations of States for military purposes, including all decisions of their legislative and executive organs on the subject. States shall periodically, within specified time-limits, furnish the control organ with information on the execution of the measures provided for in the convention (treaty).

2. *During the second stage* of execution of measures for the reduction of armaments and the prohibition of atomic weapons:

The carrying out of the measures provided for in the Declaration set forth above and of the measures for the reduction of armaments and armed forces and the prohibition of atomic and hydrogen weapons envisaged for the first stage will create the requisite atmosphere of confidence between States, thereby ensuring the necessary conditions for the extension of the functions of the international control organ.

In these circumstances, the international control organ shall have the following rights and powers:

    (a) To exercise supervision, including inspection on a continuing basis, to the extent necessary to ensure implementation of the convention by all States. In the discharge of these functions, the international control organ shall also have the right to require from States any necessary information on the execution of measures for the reduction of armaments and armed forces.

Staff recruited to carry out the work of inspection shall be selected on an international basis.

(b) To have in all States signatories to the convention its own permanent staff of inspectors, having unimpeded access at all times, within the limits of the supervisory functions they exercise, to all objects of control.

In order to prevent a surprise attack by one State upon another, the international control organ shall in particular have on the territory of all the States concerned, on a basis of reciprocity, control posts at large ports, at railway junctions, on main motor highways and in aerodromes.

(c) The control organ shall have unimpeded access to records relating to the budgetary appropriations of States for military purposes, including all decisions of their legislative and executive organs on the subject. States shall periodically, within specified time-limits, furnish the control organ with information on the execution of the measures provided for in the convention (treaty).

3. The control organ shall make recommendations to the Security Council on measures of prevention and suppression with regard to States infringing the convention on the reduction of armaments and the prohibition of atomic weapons.

4. The functions and powers of the permanent international control organ shall be defined on the basis of the foregoing principles, and appropriate instructions shall be prepared for this purpose.

U.S. VIEWS ON LATEST SOVIET DISARMAMENT PROPOSALS
Statement by James J. Wadsworth*

Now, for the third time in the subcommittee meetings this year, the Soviet Union has reversed its line and this time seems to be using ideas and language which are similar in many respects to the views put forward for many years—by Canada, France, the United Kingdom, and the United States. My immediate reaction is that ideas which have been advocated by Western powers as long ago as 1947 are at last being seriously considered by the Soviet Union.

---

*Issued at London on May 11, 1955 (press release 261). Ambassador Wadsworth is U.S. representative to the meetings of the subcommittee of the U.N. Disarmament Commission.

Clearly, our patience and persistence is paying off on some points. We welcome this development.

The Soviet Union now also seems to recognize that progress on the issue of disarmament is closely related to progress in other areas of international relations—a point the United States has long emphasized. Obviously the subcommittee was not created to deal with many of these issues, and I would therefore think it improper to comment on the wide range of problems brought in. They affect the interests of a good many states not represented in the subcommittee.

However, many questions must be asked and we hope will now be answered. For example, if we do not provide a really effective means of seeing to it that agreements reached are carried out in fact, then we will be deluding not only ourselves but all the peoples of the world who hope and long for real disarmament. In this connection, the sections of the Soviet proposals concerning international control and inspection still appear to fall short of the minimum safety requirements. It is not clear that the control organ's inspectors can go everywhere and see everything necessary to make sure that forbidden munitions are not being manufactured or that nuclear weapons are not being secreted. It will require some time before we will know what is the true Soviet position on this crucial question of controls.

The United States wants to see force and the threat of force, in all its forms, ended as an instrument of international relations. We recognize the urgency of the problem, and we recognize too its difficulty. We will neither be deterred by difficulty, nor accept shadow for substance, in a matter so gravely affecting the freedom and the security of all men.

In this spirit we will give the Soviet position the most responsible consideration.

Appendix D

Jackson's Account of the Evolution of the Open Skies Proposal

[*Note:* This appendix contains C. D. Jackson's reconstruction in August 1955 of the Open Skies initiative. (From the C. D. Jackson Papers, box 56, "Log-1955" folder, Dwight D. Eisenhower Library.)]

FROM QUANTICO TO GENEVA—June & July 1955

Went to Quantico for the opening Sunday night session on June 5th, to find the atmosphere super-charged. The State Dept. boys had ganged up against the Quantico idea as no business of outsiders, and had persuaded Herbert Hoover Jr. to persuade Foster Dulles to go to the President to kill the whole thing. Nelson Rockefeller in turn persuaded the President to persuade Foster to persuade Hoover to let Nelson have his meeting—but all of this didn't improve the atmosphere. Official Washington at the indian and one-feather-chief level was not pleased. Frank Wisner confirmed this on the telephone later when he said, "The general attitude here is one of irritation at the idea that some smart outside one-shot kibitzers will be able to suck out of their thumbs something that the professionals who work 365 days a year won't already have thought of, and probably discarded."

Nelson tried to smile his way through the gloom, and he and Rostow were quick to make disclaimers as to any intention to produce anything that could conceivably have a bearing on Geneva. This was to be long-range distant stuff, and obviously Quantico would not presume to suggest to the professionals what should happen at Geneva, on which they were already working feverishly.

Negative atmosphere further complicated by the fact that the Ph.D.'s immediately got into a semantic rhubarb over definitions of words such as "peace", and for a while it looked as though all five days would be spent arguing about definitions, with the losers sulking in corners.

Rostow's suggestion that besides conference work and conference papers, individuals should assume the responsibility of immediately producing special papers on their specialties, met with something less than enthusiasm. As a matter of fact, even I couldn't quite figure out when anybody was going to sleep.

Motored back to Washington that night with Allen Dulles and Wally Barbour of State, feeling very doubtful about the whole exercise, but having promised to return Wednesday night the 8th. During the ride back, Barbour, the stripes of whose pants glow in the dark, studiously refrained from any reference to the evening's goings-on, which added to my worries.

I had notified Colonel Kintner earlier in the week that I didn't think Nelson's idea of having the outside experts work all day and then present their findings to carefully selected Government visitors in the evening, who would come down for dinner and briefing, was a good idea—in fact, told Kintner doubted if anything would come of Quantico unless official Government participation was continuous and not on a visiting one-evening-guest basis. Kintner advised it was too late to change, which it probably was, but it later developed that Nelson's idea arose from necessity because of the virtual boycott he had run into in the Departments and Agencies.

Returned to Quantico Wednesday evening June 8th to find everybody entranced by a slide presentation by Ellis Johnson of ORO [Operations Research Office] on Soviet technical education vs U.S. engineers, the quality of Soviet end products vs the quality of U.S. end products, and a major section on U.S. continental defense, balancing various types of missiles against aircraft, against dollars, against years, against percentage of U.S. destruction.

When the lights went on, detected a completely changed atmosphere, everybody working as a team, Rostow well in command, special papers (some complete, others well in progress), and attitude, ideas, and actions at Geneva as a Quantico target. Had drinks with several of Sunday night's semantic disputants, and was delighted to find nothing but close harmony.

That evening John Baker and John Bross from CIA were the guests, and during questioning they were so CIA-cautious and double-talky that I thought important to blow this one open . . . the central point of the argument being that CIA caution made them say such things as "The intelligence community is not yet convinced that factual evidence exists to prove that the present Soviet situation is bad". My contribution was to say that if the intelligence community in the absence of a signed statement by Khrushchev could not agree that everything was not peachy in the Soviet Empire, and that the recent Soviet moves, if not from weakness, were certainly not from strength, then we might as well go home, and Eisenhower had better not go to Geneva. This came as quite a shock; Bross and Baker immediately began to backtrack, Baker later telling me that he had not meant to say what he had said, but that he couldn't say anything else in front of as large a group! But anyhow a little bit of ginger was injected.

Thursday morning to work on papers, and discovered that although the group had zeroed in on the proper target, and pulled itself together as a group, the language they were using was pure bureaucratese and had absolutely no bite whatsoever. I explained that the contribution of the Quantico group could not be simply the designation of certain selected action items, since we didn't have the staff work to war-game any particular item. We should present as many suggestions as possible, leaving it to State, Defense, AEC [Atomic Energy Commission], and White House to decide what was feasible, assuming that they would look at our papers—but that the really important contribution that Quantico could make would be to *try to convey a mood* to the President and to the Secretary of State, and that a mood could not be conveyed in bureaucratese. Everybody agreed, and we started to re-write the papers.

Interestingly, among all the action items which were being tossed on the table, there was one that everybody agreed rated real emphasis and priority—namely, an inspection angle in any disarmament discussion. Rostow had originally articulated it, and it boiled down to (a) any specific proposals for arms limitation without real inspection would be suicide; (b) why not try inspection for a year without any proposals for arms limitation, and if inspection worked, then we could go into the next phase; meanwhile we would have acquired invaluable knowledge and also possibly relaxed tensions.

Although the following is ahead of the chronological story, the following words appear in the "Report of the Quantico Vulnerabilities Panel" dated June 10, 1955:—

"IV. GENERAL PRINCIPLES OF STRATEGY.

". . . . . . (paragraph) 8. These proposals call first for the initiation of a system of mutual inspection of armaments, including forces and production facilities without, in the first instance, any provisions for arms limitation. Ultimately an inspection system, to be effective, should provide for free overflights of aircraft by reciprocally inspected aircraft, however sensitive the USSR may be on this subject."

This is further elaborated in Appendix B of the Report, as follows:

"The long-run objective of both East and West is a system of arms control and collective security on which we can all rely and in which we can all have confidence. It will take time to devise and construct such a system. At its core must lie a free exchange of information on armaments and a comprehensive system of inspection tested by trial and error.

"The following specific proposals are suggested:

"1. An agreement for mutual inspection of military installations, weapons, and armaments. Until experience has been developed on the feasibility of such inspection, this agreement would make no provision for arms limitation. Its purpose would be to provide knowledge and evidence on the basis of which a control plan could be devised.

"2. A convention insuring the right of aircraft of any nationality to fly freely over the territory of any country for peaceful purposes. The possibility of abuse of this right could be prevented by the establishment of safely located control points for the international inspection and registration of aircraft for flights across international boundaries.* The convention would be so drawn as not to interfere in any way with any nation's right to control for economic reasons commercial activities of foreign aircraft.

"*While it is assumed that all suggestions will be carefully staffed it is recommended that this particular proposal be examined thoroughly by the Department of Defense."

Despite a lot of conjecture as to who first thought of the Eisenhower Geneva bombshell on overflight inspection, the Quantico group stated it explicitly and put it in writing well ahead of Geneva. The inspection concept having been discussed Sunday and Monday at Quantico, it was Millikan who added overflight on Tuesday afternoon—he having remembered a discussion held a year before in Cambridge when the idea was played with.

Interesting sidelight was that when Hans Speier, who works for Rand, heard this, he became very perturbed and felt it was his duty to inform A-2 immediately that Quantico was about to make this suggestion. It was felt that to divulge it at that time might have ruined the whole plan, and Speier was persuaded by Possony to keep quiet. In return, Speier insisted that a footnote be inserted specifically drawing Defense Department's skeptical attention to this item. The footnote appeared in the final paper as quoted on page 3 of my log.

Managed to persuade the group to spell out Soviet vulnerabilities in simple terms of agriculture, economics, the Bomb, German rearmament, and political insecurity of the current Kremlin group, while at the same time spelling out that the Kremlin group had not lost effective control over either Russian or satellite peoples, and that their counter to their own difficulties would be forceful action to buy time, weaken NATO, get us to cut military outlays, etc.

At one moment the group got off on a "propaganda" tangent, and as chief propagandist present I took considerable pleasure in telling them that propaganda should not be a consideration of the meeting. Knowledge, mood, and action were what we should be concerned with, and if we did a good job the propaganda would take care of itself.

On the last night (June 9), a fairly large group from Washington present—[Theodore] Streibert, [Abbott] Washburn, Allen Dulles, but nobody from State. Tried very hard to get Bob Bowie, who had been reported as very sulky, but nothing doing. Nelson, who had been absent during the week, came down for the final night.

Oddly enough, Washburn precipitated my final explosion, when he out-bureaucrated the bureaucrats by a ridiculous speech on how we must be careful about London and Paris reaction, Congressional pressures, and unsureness of how our representatives at Geneva would handle themselves.

I blew up and gave him hell on U.S. leadership, and how we had been balked at every turn by London and Paris, but how London and Paris would follow if we really led—and as far as the U.S. Delegation in Geneva handling itself was concerned, I thought the President was a big boy and would know what to do. Later had correspondence with Washburn on this point.

Final morning everything seemed to be rolling along fine, and I left mid-morning to catch plane.

* * *

Nelson had asked if I could help get President and Foster Dulles to pay attention to Quantico findings, and overlook jealousy of departmental indians—so wrote to President and Foster, receiving immediate favorable reply from both. Followed up with President by sending him copy of "Smell-of-Victory" memo to Luce. This also acknowledged by the President, who said he was sending to Dulles and would discuss both Quantico and memo with Dulles immediately.

* * *

Aside from mood setting, the next important task was what the President would say to the nation before he left for Geneva, and his opening Geneva statement.

Had been asked by Nelson to draft speech for the President for the San Francisco UN 10th Anniversary ceremonies to be held June 21st. Had thought this was an opportunity for President to state bold curtain-raiser for Geneva, so drafted "Merlin" (see file) on basis of setting forth principles and announcing action based on these principles which President would call for at Geneva.

Speech was turned down by President on grounds (a) too tough, (b) didn't want to use San Francisco as curtain-raiser for Geneva. He wanted to make no reference whatsoever to Geneva in this speech. He then asked Cabot Lodge to draft something for him, which turned out to be other extreme, too wishy-washy. President then drafted his own version, sticking strictly to principles, but encompassing in those principles the ideas originally outlined in Merlin. (See Eisenhower Speeches file for final text.)

Later it was decided that the President would make a 15-minute television address to the nation just before leaving for Geneva, and Nelson got Rostow to Washington to help on this—but more importantly, to help on President's Geneva opener. Rostow reported daily on mood, which started very soft, largely due to State position papers and innocent misunderstanding between President and Dulles, President thinking Dulles simply wanted him to be Geneva M.C., with no substance, whereas Dulles worried lest President would think Geneva simply a boy scout opportunity and not get down to cases. This was a complete failure of communication which tried to remedy, and kept emphasizing to Nelson and Rostow that irrespective of what either the President or Dulles felt, the facts were that the eyes of the world would be on Eisenhower, not as an M.C. but as a principal actor in this tremendous drama; that he need not cover the entire water front, but had to be boldly substantive on at least one item.

As days went by, Rostow reported improvement in Potomac guts, although could not guarantee end product, which subject to many vicissitudes.

President's informal television appearance good, but not super. However, everything seemed on the rails.

(At this point, see log on July 11th farewell dinner with Dulles [Appendix H].)

* * *

Thought President's Geneva opener excellent, and cabled Nelson he should be very happy. When President's inspection overflight bombshell hit Thursday, Nelson cabled me I should be very happy—which I was, because I knew this was direct consequence Quantico, though didn't know at the time how it came about.

* * *

On July 25th, went to Washington with Luce, lunched with Walter Robertson, had afternoon session with Foster Dulles. . . . .

Dulles . . . quite explicit, interesting, and enormously happy about Geneva. Referred to team-play with President, said Zhukov play by Soviets a dud because he acted like automaton rather than human being, and if anybody took anybody else into camp, it was Prexy [Eisenhower] taking Zhukov. He emphasized that military had enthusiastically endorsed inspection overflight idea, which he urged us to treat as serious, feasible proposal and not as super cold war gesture. Referred to Eden being miffed, to Molotov being pretty washed out and not having an original idea or giving appearance of being able to act independently as he had in Berlin.

Tried to see Nelson that evening, but he had just returned that day from Europe and was exhausted. Agreed he would let me know when Luce and I could meet with him. Word came we were to have dinner on Wednesday, August 3rd.

* * *

August 3rd. This dinner with Rockefeller cleared up most of the points of mystery and showed how wrong the press had been on some of its guesses.

Story on overflight as follows:

Nelson, Radford, Stassen, and Bob Anderson having been told to stay out of sight in Paris and await telephonic instructions for Geneva, Nelson felt that one way of passing the time would be to organize a briefing for them on Quantico. Nelson had brought several members of his staff with him—Nancy Hanks, Steve Possony, Gen. Ted Parker, Col. Bill Kintner, Lloyd Free.

On Monday morning, Nelson had Lloyd Free give a briefing on a Gallup type survey on European opinion on the U.S., on disarmament, on nuclear warfare, etc.—all so negative that Radford was definitely perturbed. Nelson then went into the guts of the Quantico report, which fell on very deaf ears—"Radford doodled the whole time." Stassen highly sceptical because this would interfere with his peace plans, which consisted almost exclusively of giving way to Russia's May 10 proposals.

Nelson and Co. again made the point, which had originally been made in Quantico, again when Rostow was in Washington pre-Geneva helping to draft the President's opening statement, and later in Paris over the weekend—namely, that once the President had made his opener, the U.S. side was going to run out of gas because the State Department position was traditionally let's-wait-and-see-what-the-other-fellow-does; that it was essential that something plausible, feasible, and dramatic should be presented, and Nelson again started a second time round on Quantico.

At this point, Possony, feeling that Nelson was not explaining overflight inspection with sufficient clarity, interrupted and rammed it home—at which Radford came to life almost galvanically, and grabbed for it. Much discussion, including the drafting of what might be the President's statement on this.

By this time Stassen had given over and become interested.

Nelson cabled Goodpaster, Radford and Stassen cabled Dulles. Geneva responded quickly and told them to come up, but to stay out of sight in Lausanne. Nelson and his group, with Stassen, took night train Tuesday. Radford and Anderson stayed behind to brief and check with Gruenther—a very good thing as later developed.

In Switzerland, further discussion and elaboration with the President and Foster, including editing and re-editing several drafts of statement, Stassen insisting on plugging his line, Nelson editing it out (finally President wrote his own version). All agreed to keep this top secret even from lower rank Americans.

However, President decided to tell Eden but not the French. Eden wanted military estimate of this, and asked that Gruenther be brought to Geneva, as he did not know Radford that well. Gruenther quickly summoned with Anderson and Radford. By the time Gruenther reached Geneva, he was an articulate and enthusiastic salesman for the plan.

President kept up his sleeve for right moment, which occurred on Thursday, Bulganin's day to preside.

Normally presiding officer opens session by turning clockwise or counterclockwise, as case may be, and asking next Delegate to make first speech. Contrary to precedent, Bulganin launched into a rehash of the earlier Soviet disarmament position, which made the President realize that the moment was now. So he started reading his normal paper and then took off his glasses and uttered the famous 300 words.

Nelson reports that the impact was absolutely terrific. He didn't subscribe to Foster's theory, or newspaper reports, that Eden was miffed. Eden had known and approved, and according to Nelson handled the reprise of the Eden Plan very gracefully. Very disappointed to hear that several of the lesser State Department characters, led, unfortunately, by Bob Bowie, were most miffed of all. When I asked Nelson why, he replied, "It wasn't in the position papers".

Quantico-Geneva—long and complicated, but good payoff.

P.S. Considering the inauspicious start of Quantico, and the number of natural born enemies, it is a near-miracle that no leak whatsoever occurred.

Appendix E

Ted Parker's Assembly of Documents on the
Evolution of the Open Skies Proposal

[*Note:* Ted Parker's valuable chronology is included in the text (see pp. 34–36, above). Most of the documents bearing on the summit mutual inspection proposal that he assembled are included in this appendix. The documents not included here are either repetitive or are covered adequately in the text. (From papers personally released for publication by Nelson Rockefeller.)]

OFFICE MEMORANDUM   UNITED STATES GOVERNMENT

TO: Nelson A. Rockefeller   DATE: August 3, 1955
FROM: General Parker   INFORMATION MEMORANDUM
SUBJECT: Chronology of Mutual Inspection Proposal

Attached is a copy for your file of "how the mutual inspection proposal came to be made."

No action is planned with respect to this paper. It was prepared simply to have the accurate record on hand for history's sake.

Attachment
As stated.

TO: Nelson A. Rockefeller   DATE: June 30, 1955
FROM: General Parker   ACTION MEMORANDUM
SUBJECT: Disarmament Plan

The NSC meeting today was devoted almost entirely to a discussion of a U.S. plan for disarmament.* This subject is of outstanding importance because:

* A single copy synopsis of the discussion is attached (to be destroyed after reading).

129

1. It is so closely related to the establishment of lasting peace, our primary long-term objective.

2. Our former U.S. position is outmoded and we have not developed a new one.

3. The Soviets are almost certain to press discussion of this subject at the Geneva Big-Four Conference.

4. The Soviets have the initiative in this field by virtue of their 10 May 1955 proposals which represented, for them, great concessions.

5. More than any other world problem, it has universal appeal and decided psychological aspects.

6. If we come to a wrong position, we will sacrifice our security either through loss of our allies or loss of the strength with which to defend ourselves.

The next step directed by the President is a study by Gov. Stassen to determine a workable, satisfactory inspection method, if such exists. This will take some time, and, in fact, it was agreed that it should not be hurried. It will not be ready for use at Geneva.

Had you been present at the NSC meeting today, I believe you would have offered the recommendation, which was included in the Quantico Vulnerabilities Panel Report, that the U.S. propose an agreement for mutual inspection of military installations, forces, and armaments, without limitations provisions. I believe that, as a matter of urgency, you should still offer the President, Gov. Stassen and Secretary Dulles this recommendation. It seemed to me today that throughout the discussion three points stood out:

1. Inspection is the key to disarmament.

2. We must have something we can talk about.

3. We must educate the people as to what a satisfactory disarmament plan entails.

The proposal for testing an inspection system *before* disarming seems to be a step in the direction of meeting all three points. I cannot see any aspect of it—even if the Soviets accept it, which would be a great surprise to me—which in any way seriously jeopardizes our security. Instead, it would offer many advantages other than the main one of testing to determine the practicability of an inspection system. Among the collateral advantages:

1. Regains the initiative in disarmament negotiation; provides us a position at Geneva.

2. Helps break down the Iron Curtain.

3. Provides us intelligence.

4. Poses a difficult decision for Soviets.

5. Focuses on a practical and immediate aspect of disarmament which people in general can understand.

6. Exposes the phoniness of the proposed Soviet inspection system—the Korean-like type that provides for international inspectors at ports, major airfields, etc.

7. Demonstrates first hand to the Soviets our greater war potential.

RECOMMENDATION

That you recommend orally to the President, Secretary Dulles, and Gov. Stassen that consideration be given to proposing at Geneva an agreement for mutual inspection of military installations, forces, and armaments, without limitations provisions; this action to be taken in addition to the study Gov. Stassen has been directed to make to develop the inspection system part of his plan.

TAB A

*Extracts from Report of the Quantico Vulnerabilities Panel
10 June 1955*

From Section IV, GENERAL PRINCIPLES OF THE STRATEGY, paragraph 4, page 10:

Even more important, the world has hanging over it the shadow of destructive nuclear warfare, which, as Mr. Malenkov has rightly said, could destroy modern civilization. We shall leave no stone unturned in the pursuit of ways to effect a real reduction in this threat. We have a series of proposals we should make at the appropriate time for taking what we believe to be constructive first steps toward a system of arms limitation. As explained in more detail in Appendix D, we are prepared to accept certain of the May 10 proposals of the Soviets; for example, a reduction of ground forces. We have proposals for the development of a workable inspection system for control of armaments. We also have proposals for considering alleviation of the effects of radioactive fall-out.

From the same section, paragraph 8, page 12:

With respect to the control of armaments, we should emphasize that some degree of understanding and even trust is essential to any effective armaments control scheme. We suggest a series of proposals for the control of armaments which take into account the Russian proposals of May 10, 1955. Our proposals also look to the improvement of relations and the free exchange of people, ideas, and goods. These proposals call first for the initiation of a system of mutual inspection of armaments, including forces and production facilities without, in the first instance, any provisions for arms limitation. Ultimately, an inspection system, to be effective, should provide for free overflights of aircraft by reciprocally inspected aircraft, however sensitive the USSR may be on this subject.* Proposals also include those for an expansion of economic relations and for free exchange of information and ideas, both by the flow of written materials and by unobstructed radio broadcasting, and a proposal for the freer access of persons to all countries. These are all spelled out in more detail in Appendixes B and D.

From Section V, *RECOMMENDATIONS*, Part B, *Actions During the Conference*, paragraph 1, page 13:

The United States should be prepared to make a series of proposals designed to move towards the control of armaments. These include:

a. Discussions of:

(1) A proposed agreement for mutual inspection of military installations, forces, and armaments, without limitations provisions. (Appendix B)

(2) A convention insuring the right of aircraft of any nationality to fly over the territory of any country for peaceful purposes. (Proposed with reservations noted in the text. See Appendix B.)

b. Proposal of a disarmament plan to the USSR (Appendix D); after rejection of the plan, the U.S. to make every effort to win the arms race as the safest way of forcing the Soviet Union to accept a satisfactory arms convention.

From Appendix B, *Proposals to Test Soviet Willingness to Make Concessions And to Improve the U.S. Position*, paragraph 1, page 1:

---

* Note: Aside from our general assumption that before implementation all these suggestions will be considered carefully by the Departments, it is recommended that this proposal be examined with particular skepticism by the Department of Defense.

An agreement for mutual inspection of military installations, weapons, and armaments. Until experience has been developed on the feasibility of such inspection, this agreement would make no provision for arms limitation. Its purpose would be to provide knowledge and evidence on the basis of which a control plan could be devised.

From Appendix D, *A PROPOSAL FOR GRADUATED DISARMA-MENT*, page 6:

A disarmament plan would need to be put into effect gradually. Accordingly, a relatively safe disarmament plan could be based on the following guiding ideas:

1. A permanent disarmament commission would be established to survey continuously new requirements rising from changing military technology. The basic armament convention will be revised annually so that it will be continuously up to date.

2. An inspection system is instituted on an experimental basis to determine methods and requirements of, and to train personnel for a dependable inspection system including aerial supervision.

TAB B

July 6, 1955

MEMORANDUM FOR THE PRESIDENT

SUBJECT: Disarmament Proposal for Four Power Conference

Basic U.S. policies, with exception of disarmament, are considered in NSC 5524, Basic U.S. Policy in Relation to Four Power Conference, which is up for consideration Thursday, July 7. The U.S. position on disarmament, which was studied separately by Governor Stassen, was considered at last Thursday's NSC meeting. As a result of that consideration, you directed Governor Stassen to study further and in detail the problem of inspection to determine if a workable, satisfactory inspection method exists and, if so, how it affects his plan. The results of this study will not be available for the Big Four conference.

The subject of disarmament is of outstanding importance in connection with preparations for the Big Four conference because:

1. It is so closely related to the establishment of lasting peace, our primary long-term objective.

2. Our former U.S. position is outmoded and we have not developed a new one.

3. The Soviets are almost certain to press discussion of this subject at the Geneva Big Four conference.

4. The Soviets have the initiative in this field by virtue of their May 10, 1955, proposals which represented, for them, great concessions.

5. More than any other world problem it has universal appeal and decided psychological aspects.

6. If we come to a wrong position, we will sacrifice our security either through loss of our allies or loss of the strength with which to defend ourselves.

In last week's NSC discussion of disarmament three main points stood out:

1. Inspection is the key to disarmament.

2. We must have something we can talk about.

3. We must educate the people as to what a satisfactory disarmament entails.

I believe that you should give serious consideration to the proposal on the part of the U.S. at the forthcoming conference for an agreement for mutual inspection of military installations, forces and armaments without limitations provisions. This proposal for testing an inspection system before limiting or reducing armaments seems to me to be a step in the direction of meeting all three points I have listed above. I cannot see any aspect of it—even if the Soviets accept it, which is highly doubtful—which in any way seriously jeopardizes our security. Instead, it would offer many advantages beyond the main one of testing to determine the practicability of an inspection system. Among the collateral advantages are the following:

1. Regains the initiative in disarmament negotiation; provides us a position at Geneva.

2. Helps break down the Iron Curtain.

3. Provides us intelligence.

4. Poses a difficult decision for the Soviets.

5. Focuses on a practical and immediate aspect of disarmament which people in general can understand.

6. Exposes the phoniness of the proposed Soviet inspection

system—the Korean-like type that provides for international inspectors at ports, major airfields, etc.

7. Demonstrates first hand to the Soviets our greater war potential.

RECOMMENDATION

That, subject to concurrence of the Secretary of State, the Secretary of Defense, and Governor Stassen, and, further, subject to coordination with the British and the French, you offer at the forthcoming Big Four conference a proposal for mutual inspection of military installations, forces, and armaments, without any arms limitations provisions.

Nelson A. Rockefeller

TAB E

Draft of Anderson-Radford Message to Dulles, 19 July 1955
(First paragraph only.)

Our analysis of the four opening statements while perhaps not presenting basic ideas which have not already occurred to you leads us to suggest the following: Throughout the Soviet statement repeated references are made to the banning of atomic weapons but no suggestion is made as to the practical accomplishment of this objective which obviously can not be realistic merely from the standpoint of international declaration. It would seem desirable to emphasize as a matter of amplification of the President's statement the necessity for exploring the possibilities of effective inspections by the principals involved as a necessary prelude to any armaments control, emphasizing also that armaments control of necessity includes the whole of conventional and nonconventional weapons which separate parts can not be isolated. The establishment of an appropriate group to explore inspection mechanism perhaps proceeding from the most elementary to the more complex would appear to be an affirmative proposal designed to determine the good faith of all concerned and is much more realistic than the Faure proposal of budgetary control which would always be subject to national systems of accounting which are both unique to the several countries and which are susceptible to change and manipulation.

July 19, 1955

FROM: PARIS
TO: GENEVA
For Colonel Andrew Goodpaster, US Delegation to
Conference from Nelson Rockefeller

Following draft statement is submitted for consideration and possible use of President in subsequent discussion of armaments question. From psychological and public opinion point of view President laid excellent foundation on subject of limitation of armaments in opening statement Monday. It appears highly desirable to expand on this foundation by explaining in greater detail what is meant by supervision and inspection. Lack of Allied unity on disarmament question highlights necessity of U.S. asserting leadership to demonstrate clearly to people of Western nations the key aspect of supervision and inspection by spelling it out in simple terms and putting it squarely up to Soviets.

This draft statement has been written in a conciliatory tone but in a manner to sharpen the issue.

The basic principles of this statement were developed through our group conferences of Stassen, Anderson and Radford. They are reflected in paragraph one of the Anderson-Radford message to the Secretary of State, dated 19 July.

The particular statement represents our suggestions as to the psychological strategy for handling the matter. The draft has been reviewed by the group and contains Stassen's specific suggestions and has his endorsement.

PRESIDENTIAL STATEMENT ON DISARMAMENT

Mr. Chairman: I have given much thought to the initial views expressed by the heads of governments at this conference. Evidently we all recognize that excessive armaments impede progress toward security and a just peace.

It was very interesting to me that each delegation approached the security problem in a different manner. The various proposals do not differ in every detail and some of the differences undoubtedly are due to the particularities of each country's defense requirements. However, these differences are sufficiently vast that they indicate, to me at least, that the complexity of the security problem has not really been fully understood. We owe it to ourselves, and to the world, that we admit this fact without ambiguity.

The various proposals made concerning security can, to my mind, be divided into four broad types. Some deal with the problems of mutual security relating to the re-unification of Germany and, in various ways, suggest limitations on the armed forces stationed in the German area. Some deal with the connected problem of a general European security arrangement. Some are directed toward world-wide levels of total armaments. Others concern nuclear weapons.

It seems to me that if we ever are to arrive at a suitable, secure and dependable arrangement for safeguarding the peace we must proceed on a positive basis, one step at a time. On a matter as important as disarmament I do not think that it would be in the interest of any one of us to plunge into a venture the result of which might heighten rather than lessen tensions. To avoid raising misleading hopes, each step we make toward a system of arms limitations must be well thought out in advance. No subsequent step should be taken until the preceding move has been tried, proven and found mutually acceptable. If we were to act differently, we would all gamble with the security of our people. The hopes which the people of the world have for peace must rest on a truly solid foundation. The structure of peace cannot be built on sand.

We will not serve humanity by discussing now security arrangements which would be unenforceable and would only result in increasing fears. Ultimately, we hope that through our mutual efforts the time will come sooner or later when a real solution to the general security problem will come into sight.

In listening to the proposals being made the first day I kept searching for a common thread which would bring us closer together. As the list of specific suggestions grew—the freeze on troops stationed in foreign countries, the prohibition of atomic weapons, the demobilization of forces withdrawn from occupation duty, agreements on the levels of conventional forces, reduction of armaments through budgetary control and economic development programs, the limitation of forces in Germany and adjacent countries, the creation of demilitarized zones, and others—it became obvious to me that the dependable success of each one of them required that our priority task is to develop an effective, workable, supervision and inspection system.

We might sign agreements on paper to limit forces. We might sign pledges to ban atomic weapons or to demobilize some of our forces. We might construct the most intricate web of inter-related—and let me be frank—sometimes contradictory security pacts. However, without a reciprocal means of observing whether these agreements were being complied with, we would actually be working in the dark. There would not be—there could not be—any real security, unless each of us knows what the other nation is actually doing.

Once and for all we must discard the deceptive notion that paper agreements or promises on matters as vital as our national security can have any real value. The experiences which we all shared in the years preceding the last great war should have taught us this basic lesson.

Now, since it is true that workable inspection is the key and the indispensable pre-condition to all meaningful security proposals, it follows that we should concentrate initially on the problem of supervision and inspection.

But, again, it is easy to formulate all sorts of vague inspection proposals. But what we must take as the indispensable first step, if we are really to begin to ban the danger of war, is a truly workable and effective system of mutual inspection.

How can we develop such a system of inspection to which, in one form or another, the heads of the four governments have referred as one of the significant problems? The first essential is a real desire to move ahead. Mutual assurances are indispensable if international tensions are to be relaxed. But how do we evidence their validity? We can only test their validity through the hard but rewarding methods of the engineer.

One of the basic elements of control is the inspection of efforts each of us are making in the security area. This introduces a very unique problem. I believe one of our first tasks is to see what we can do in the simple fields. If we are successful there, we can increase our efforts with the more complex problems.

As a concrete beginning let us draw up a plan for a testing machinery for inspection of military installations. We must then test this original blueprint on a small scale and gradually proceed to larger models. Experience will reveal weak points and suggest modifications. We shall have to redraw our blueprints time and again until we all shall be satisfied that at least we have fashioned a key which can open the door to a secure peace. Only when this stage will have arrived, only after we have concluded a treaty on this system, can we install inspection machinery which will enable us to adopt and put into effect many of the excellent suggestions that have been made here. The United States is prepared to embark on this venture.

This may seem like a slow process. But it is my profound conviction that we will advance much faster toward our goal than by any other way. More important, by being systematic and scientific we will go much further on the real road to peace. Any thought that we can improve the situation by turning the clock back twenty years has been vitiated by the momentous political and technological changes which have occurred since the beginning of World War II.

I propose that we refer the task of designing a mutually acceptable inspection system to the group of experts who, in the U.N. Subcommittee on Disarmament, have dealt with this question for many years.

I propose, that we explore together the requirements for a machinery of effective, mutual inspection, with the initial objective of seeking dependable ways to supervise and inspect military establishments in our respective countries.

This exploration should be conducted in two broad areas. One would be between those nations possessing global military forces. The other would involve those nations having regional forces in Europe and perhaps elsewhere.

We may find it initially desirable to institute the inspection system at only a few military establishments at a time, increasing the number as we perfect our methods and develop confidence in the results we achieve—and in each other.

Inspection teams should also be free to overfly the territory of the nation being inspected, in order to determine by aerial observation the location and activity of military establishments in its territory and to make sure that none remains hidden.

To do their job each inspection team must possess reliable communications to its home nation, and concurrently, if desirable, to such international headquarters as the United Nations. It is through such realistic methods that we can all reduce the fear of surprise attack.

All this shall be done, I propose, for the purpose of devising and testing dependable basis on which real and lasting progress can be made in the limitation of armaments. We must learn to walk before we can run.

This is a bold but at the same time utterly realistic proposal for reciprocal inspections. It strikes at the root of our distrust—the fear of what we do not know. If we go along this road we shall be demonstrating to our citizens, and in fact to all the peoples of the world who will be watching our labors with fervent hope, that many complex problems must be solved in order to build the kind of effective inspection machinery which can make possible real and beneficial arms agreement.

The quest for peace is the statesman's most exacting duty. Security of the nations entrusted to his care is his greatest responsibility. Practical progress to lasting peace is his fondest hope. Yet we must not betray the trust placed in us as guardians of our people's security. A sound peace *can* be achieved but only on the basis of mutual knowledge as well as mutual goodwill. Only by following this hard but sure road to peace can we achieve our eventual goals of security, justice, well-being and freedom for all the people of the world.

TAB G
Draft of Statement of President Eisenhower
on the Subject of Disarmament

Mr. Chairman, Gentlemen:

The statements made in this session and on the preceding days of this conference on the subject of disarmament by each of you have been followed by me with close interest.

It is the most important subject on our agenda. It is also the most difficult. In recent years the scientists have discovered methods of making weapons many, many times more destructive of opposing armed forces, but also of homes, and industries, and lives, than ever known or even imagined before. These same scientific discoveries have made more complex the problems of limitation and control and reduction of armament.

After our common victory in World War II, my country rapidly disarmed. Within a few years our armament was at a very low level. Then events occurred beyond our borders which caused us to realize that we had disarmed too much. For our own security and to safeguard peace we needed greater strength. Therefore we proceeded to rearm and to associate with others in a partnership for peace and mutual security.

My country is prepared to maintain and if necessary increase this armed strength for a long period of years if this is necessary to safeguard peace and to maintain our security.

But we also know that a mutually dependable system for less armament on the part of all nations would be a better way to safeguard peace and to maintain our security.

It would ease the fears of war in the anxious hearts of people everywhere. It would lighten the burdens upon the backs of the people. It would make possible for every nation, great and small, developed and less developed, to advance the standard of living of its people, to attain better food, clothing, and shelter, more of education and larger enjoyment of life.

Therefore my government is prepared to enter into a sound and reliable agreement for less armament. I have directed that an intensive and thorough study of this subject be made. From these studies, which are continuing, a very important principle is emerging to which I referred in my opening statement on Monday. No sound and reliable agreement can be made unless it is completely covered by an inspection and reporting system adequate to support every portion of the agreement.

The lessons of history teach us that disarmament agreements without inspection increase the dangers of war and do not brighten the prospects of peace.

Thus it is my view that the priority focus of our combined study of disarmament should be upon the subject of inspection and reporting. How effective an inspection system can be designed which would be mutually and reciprocally acceptable within our countries and the other nations of the world? How would such a system operate? What could it accomplish? Is complete certainty against surprise aggression attainable by inspection? Could important violations be discovered promptly and effectively counteracted?

We have not as yet been able to discover any scientific or other inspection method which would make certain of the elimination of nuclear weapons and would be interested in knowing if any other nation has made such a discovery. Our study of this problem is continuing. We have not as yet been able to discover any accounting or other inspection method of being certain of the true budgetary costs of total armament. Our study of this problem is continuing.

As you can see from these statements, it is our impression that many, if not all, past proposals of disarmament are more widespread than can be covered by the inspection methods suggested.

From my statements I believe you will anticipate my suggestion. It is that we instruct our representatives in the UN Subcommittee on Disarmament to give priority attention to the study of inspection and reporting. Such a study could well include a step by step testing of inspection and reporting methods.

I announce to you now that for the purposes of designing and testing an inspection and reporting system which will serve this magnificent objective of disarmament and peace, my government is ready in principle to permit trial inspection of units of our armed forces if other countries will do the same. My government is ready in principle to test inspection on the ground in specified comparable zones if other countries will do the same.

We are ready to proceed in the study and testing of a reliable system of inspections and reporting, and when that system is designed then to reduce armaments together to the extent that the system will provide assured results.

This exploration could be conducted in two broad areas. One could be between those nations possessing global military forces. The other could involve those nations having regional forces in Europe or elsewhere.

The successful working out of such a system would do much to develop the mutual confidence which will open wide the avenues of progress for all our peoples.

The quest for peace is the statesman's most exacting duty. Security of the nations entrusted to his care is his greatest responsibility. Practical progress to lasting peace is his fondest hope. Yet we must not betray the trust placed in us as guardians of our people's security. A sound peace *can* be achieved but only on the basis of mutual knowledge as well as mutual good will. Only by following this hard but sure road to peace can we achieve our eventual goals of security, justice, well-being, and freedom for all the people of the world.

TAB H
EISENHOWER ARMS TEXT

Mr. Chairman, gentlemen:

Disarmament is one of the most important subjects on our agenda. It is also extremely difficult. In recent years the scientists have discovered methods of making weapons many, many times more destructive of opposing armed forces—but also of homes, and industries and lives—than even known or even imagined before.

These same scientific discoveries have made much more complex the problems of limitation and control and reduction of armament.

After our victory as allies in World War II, my country rapidly disarmed. Within a few years our armament was at a very low level. Then events occurred beyond our borders which caused us to realize that we had disarmed too much. For our own security and to safeguard peace we needed greater strength. Therefore we proceeded to rearm and to associate with others in a partnership for peace and for mutual security.

The American people are determined to maintain and if necessary increase this armed strength for as long a period as is necessary to safeguard peace and to maintain our security.

But we know that a mutually dependable system for less armament on the part of all nations would be a better way to safeguard peace and to maintain our security.

It would ease the fears of war in the anxious hearts of people everywhere. It would lighten the burdens upon the backs of the people. It would make it possible for every nation, large and small, developed and less developed, to advance the standards of living of its people, to attain better food and clothing and shelter, more of education and larger enjoyment of life.

Therefore, the United States Government is prepared to enter into a sound and reliable agreement making possible the reduction of armament. I have directed that an intensive and thorough study of this subject be made within our own Government. From these studies, which are continuing, a very important principle is emerging to which I referred in my opening statement on Monday.

No sound and reliable agreement can be made unless it is completely covered by an inspection and reporting system adequate to support every portion of the agreement.

The lessons of history teach us that disarmament agreements without adequate reciprocal inspection increase the dangers of war and do not brighten the prospects of peace.

Thus it is my view that the priority attention of our combined study of disarmament should be upon the subject of inspection and reporting.

Questions suggest themselves.

How effective an inspection system can be designed which would be mutually and reciprocally acceptable within our countries and the other nations of the world? How would such a system operate? What could it accomplish?

Is certainty against surprise aggression attainable by inspection? Could violations be discovered promptly and effectively counteracted?

We have not as yet been able to discover any scientific or other inspection method which would make certain of the elimination of nuclear weapons. So far as we are aware no other nation has made such a discovery. Our study of this problem is continuing. We have not as yet been able to discover any accounting or other inspection method of being certain of the true budgetary facts of total expenditures for armament. Our study of this problem is continuing. We by no means exclude the possibility of finding useful checks in these fields.

As you can see from these statements, it is our impression that many past proposals of disarmament are more sweeping than can be insured by effective inspection.

Gentlemen, since I have been working on this memorandum to

present to this conference, I have been searching my heart and mind for something that I could say here that could convince everyone of the great sincerity of the United States in approaching this problem of disarmament.

I should address myself for a moment principally to the delegates from the Soviet Union, because our two great countries admittedly possess new and terrible weapons in quantities which do give rise in other parts of the world, or reciprocally, to the fears and danger of surprise attack.

I propose, therefore, that we take a practical step, that we begin an arrangement, very quickly, as between ourselves—immediately. These steps would include:

To give to each other a complete blueprint of our military establishments, from beginning to end, from one end of our countries to the other: lay out the establishments and provide the blueprints to each other.

Next, to provide within our countries facilities for aerial photography to the other country—we to provide you the facilities within our country, ample facilities for aerial reconnaissance, where you can make all the pictures you choose and take them to your own country to study; you to provide exactly the same facilities for us and we to make these examinations, and by this step to convince the world that we are providing as between ourselves against the possibility of great surprise attack, thus lessening danger and relaxing tensions.

Likewise we will make more easily attainable a comprehensive and effective system of inspection and disarmament, because what I propose, I assure you, would be but a beginning.

Now from my statements I believe you will anticipate my suggestion. It is that we instruct our representatives in the subcommittee on disarmament in discharge of their mandate from the United Nations to give priority effort to the study of inspection and reporting. Such a study could well include a step by step testing of inspection and reporting methods.

The United States is ready to proceed in the study and testing of a reliable system of inspections and reporting. And when that system is proved, then to reduce armaments with all others to the extent that the system will provide assured results.

The successful working out of such a system would do much to develop the mutual confidence which will open wide the avenues of progress for all our peoples.

The quest for peace is the statesman's most exacting duty. Security of the nation entrusted to his care is his greatest responsibility. Practical progress to lasting peace is his fondest hope. Yet in pursuit of his hope he must not betray the trust placed in him as guardian of the people's security. A sound peace—with security, justice, well-being, and freedom for the people of the world—can be achieved, but only by patiently and thoughtfully following a hard and sure and tested road.

Appendix F

Ellis Johnson's Analysis of Narrowing U.S.-Soviet Military Capabilities

[*Note:* Ellis Johnson's paper on U.S.-Soviet gaps in military technology, along with other comparative analyses, strongly influenced members of the Quantico Panel. (From the report of Quantico Panel I in the author's files.)]

Annex A to Tab 2 of
Report of Quantico
Vulnerabilities Panel
Dr. E. A. Johnson

*THE COMPARATIVE MILITARY TECHNOLOGY OF
THE US AND USSR*

The Problem
The problem is to establish the relative status and trends of US vs. USSR military technology.

Facts
Immediately following World War II, W. B. Shockley surveyed the technological advancement of the two countries and presented his findings in a memorandum dated 30 January 1946.* The objective of the Shockley study and of the current one is to determine the existence of the time lags in the introduction of new military items as indicators of the current and future relative positions of the US and USSR in research and technological development.

* "Relative Technological Achievement in Weapon Characteristics in the US and USSR," Memorandum, Office of the Secretary of War, 30 January 1946.

The method introduced by Shockley is followed in large measure in a study by ORO [Operations Research Office], ORO-T-322. This is directed to determining the time lag or lead in the introduction of new items or of particular characteristics of weapons judged militarily desirable by the U.S. and the USSR. In this approach, the probabilistic future work of the research and development agencies is excluded from consideration since it is impossible to identify which developments will actually culminate in successful application. Progress and trends shown by *actual* introduction of end items is a better measure of the relative state of the technology of the two countries.

Where data for a specific item permit, US and USSR achievements are charted on a time scale basis and the chart provides the pattern of time lag for a particular weapon characteristic. The composite pictures of time lag patterns for the several characteristics of specific weapons are then subject to analysis as to over-all comparability of US and USSR achievements in technology.

Lack of substantive data on USSR military items and disparities in US and USSR development programs during the 1945–1955 period have necessitated a more general interpretation of less specific evidence in some instances than in Shockley's study. This is true, for example, in the area of electronics. Available information on USSR achievements together with data on US achievements provide a basis for general conclusions as to time lag between the two countries. There are not sufficient supporting data on USSR electronics to warrant a time scale comparison of the developments in the two countries. For armor, there are only fragmentary pieces of intelligence on developments in the USSR. As of 1954–55, assumptions based on limited evidence represent the only basis for comparison of USSR tank developments with US developments.

In two respects, 1945–46 was a more propitious time than 1954–55 to make such an analysis and to obtain reliable indicators. The first applies to the accessibility and reliability of data. At the close of World War II, the US military services had possession of sufficient data pertaining to Russian weapons achievements to assure valid comparisons with US achievements. At the present time, the extent of reliable data from the USSR is indeed limited. UN intelligence estimates represent the bulk of our current information on Russian achievements. The tight Soviet security cloak may well have hidden advancements which would be particularly pertinent in a comparison of technological achievements. Estimates of dates for production and operational use of USSR equipment may be considerably later ones than the true dates.

The second factor in timing that favors the 1945–46 over the 1954–55 study pertains to the opportunity for national choice in the selection of and emphasis on specific developments during the period covered. During World War II the US and the USSR directed their national scientific and technological effort toward the single objective of winning a war. Hence, technological effort was largely expended on weapons and the development of these weapons served as a valid index of the technological potential of the nations, as analyzed by Dr. Shockley in 1946.

The past ten years has been a period of so-called peace and the focus of weapons development in the US and USSR has been less consistent. The emphasis on military research and development has been geared to the national requirements established for the respective military programs. For example, the Russians placed greater emphasis on the development of fighter planes at a time when Americans were stressing bomber developments. In general, the Soviets have not put much effort on marginal improvements with the intent that simplicity and numbers offset possible benefits to be gained from further refinement. The US on the other hand has emphasized the need for research to meet specific and detailed requirements such as safety measures for the protection of personnel, in aircraft, tanks, etc.

This element of choice reflected in the over-all programs and in specific developments makes it difficult to compare directly currently available data on US and USSR technological achievements. A comparison of the specific characteristics in the development of a single weapon must allow for a greater number of influencing factors than was the case in 1945–46.

For example, in the absence of immediate requirements for US aircraft to excel in any specific area, the US has chosen to trade other performance for range in both its fighters and bombers. Hence, the US is found to have a comparative technological advantage for this characteristic and corresponding lags for other characteristics. In this case, both the lead in fighter range and the lags in fighter speed and rate of climb may be regarded as the result of US choice. In tanks, the USSR has adopted the diesel engine that provides far greater combat range for the USSR tanks than the gasoline engine provides for US tanks. This difference in range capability is the result of choice.

Weakness in U.S. development is so much due to poor choice as any other factor and the elements of choices should be reviewed. It may be that one of the major values of a study of comparative technological achievements is the clues it provides toward pointing up shortcomings in our own design philosophy.

Notwithstanding possible discrepancies in the data, the indeterminate factors related to the element of choice, and the limited number of items covered, the comparisons of achievements presented in this study are considered to be sufficiently representative of time lag trends to serve as indicators of the relative status of technological developments in the US and the USSR. The consideration of validity is supported by the inclusion of an analysis of the most controlling factor of all research, development and production capabilities in both the US and USSR—that is the volume and rate of development of scientific and technical manpower in the two countries. The analysis of this factor contributes to the analyses of weapons characteristics and the deductions on technological development.

Comparisons of the relative development status of the US and the USSR for the specific items included in this study in the mid-forties and the mid-fifties are presented in Table 1, grouped under headings "aircraft", "armor", "ordnance", "electronics", and "scientific and technical personnel". This table represents a general summary drawn from the lag-times on a large number of items covered in ORO-T-322.

Conclusions

On balance, the Soviet military technology had a lag of about three years behind the US at the close of WWII *, but by 1954 this lag had been eliminated and the Soviet Union is now at least our equal in military technology especially in the air and on the land. Within the past decade the Soviets not only caught up to the US but

---

* The weighting includes Shockley's conclusions that the USSR in 1946 was "at least 5 years behind the US" in oil refining capability with a development rate of one-half the US rate.

in some cases passed us. The trend is such as to indicate over-all superiority of Soviet military technology in the not too distant future. This prediction is based not only upon specific achievement rates in military end items but upon the volume and rate of increase of USSR scientific and technical personnel and labor force which is now approaching numerical equality with that of the US and is increasing at a rate at least 50% faster.

Recommendations

The recommendations are implicit in the conclusions. With our present level of research and development effort the US since WWII has lost a three-year lead and the trend indicates a future over-all superiority of Soviet military technology unless actions are taken to strengthen our own and NATO research efforts in funds, management, and personnel. By support of NATO science we can add almost immediately a great new reservoir of skill to the US-NATO system.

TABLE 1. (Summary Table) Estimated Lag-Time in Scientific and Technological Developments, USSR

	Mid-1950s			Mid-1940s		
	Year	Lagging Country	Estimated Time Lag	Year	Lagging Country	Estimated Time Lag
AIRCRAFT						
Aircraft Engines						
Turboprops—estimated shaft horsepower	1955	US	6 mos behind	1952	US	1½ yrs behind
Turbojets—centrifugal compressors—thrust	1952	USSR	3 mos behind	1949	US–USSR	equal
Turboprops—axial compressors—thrust	1954	US	3 yrs behind	1949	US	1⅓ yrs behind
Jet Fighters						
Combat radius	1954	USSR	4 yrs behind	1948	US	6 mos behind
Thrust	1955	USSR	1½ yrs behind	1947	US–USSR	equal
Weight/Thrust ratio	1954	US	6 yrs behind	1947	US–USSR	equal
Service ceiling	1955	US	2½ yrs behind	1949	US–USSR	equal
Rate of climb at sea level	1954	US	4¾ yrs behind	1948	US	4 mos behind
Speed in level flight at 30,000 ft.	1954	US	3¾ yrs behind	1948	US	1 yr behind
Time to climb to 30,000 ft.	1954	US	5 yrs behind	1948	US	9 mos behind
Bomber Aircraft						
Jet light bombers—Initial Production	1951	USSR	2 yrs behind			

Item	1955 comparison			Earlier comparison		
bombers—Initial Production	1954	USSR	3 yrs behind			
Heavy bombers—Initial Production	1954	US–USSR	equal			
Aircraft Guns	1953	US–USSR	equal			
ORDNANCE				1945	USSR ranging from 2 yrs behind to 2 yrs ahead of US	
Antiaircraft Guns	1955	US–USSR	equal			
Ground rockets	1955	US lag				
Ground missiles	1955	—				
ARMOR						
Firepower						
Hit Probability	1955	US–USSR	equal (marginal)			
Penetration	1955	USSR	equal			
Mobility						
Weight	1955	US	(15–20% disadvantage)	1944	US	3½ yrs behind*
Maneuverability	1955	USSR	(marginal)	1944	US	
Range	1955	US	(2–1% disadvantage)	1944	US	
Armor Protection	1955	US–USSR	equal		US	*1½ to 2 yrs behind
Slope	1955	USSR–US	equal			
Quality	1955	USSR	(marginal)			
ELECTRONICS	1955	USSR	Ranging from 0–2 yrs behind	1945	USSR	*At least 2 yrs behind

	Mid-1950s			Mid-1940s		
	Year	Lagging Country	Estimated Time Lag	Year	Lagging Country	Estimated Time Lag
SCIENTIFIC AND TECHNICAL PERSONNEL						
Professional, Technical and Kindred Workers	1953	US lag		1945	USSR lag	
Graduates of Institutions of Higher Learning	1956	US lag		1945	USSR lag	
Professionally Active Engineers	1953	USSR lag		1945	USSR lag	
Engineering Graduates	1954	US lag		1948	US–USSR	equal

* Shockley op cit.

Appendix G

Post-Quantico Letter to Rockefeller from the Author, June 17, 1955

[*Note:* The author's letter to Rockefeller in the wake of the Quantico I Panel looks ahead over the next decade.]

June 17, 1955

Mr. Nelson Rockefeller
The White House
Washington, D.C.
Dear Mr. Rockefeller:

The week's effort at Quantico had a very particular effect on my thought and feeling which I should like to try and convey. I now, for the first time, really see how the cold war can be won within the next ten years. It can be won without American initiation of major war; and we can put ourselves and the Free World in a position of such strength as to make it extremely unlikely that the enemy will risk major war, even in the kind of acute internal crisis likely to mark the climax of the cold war.

1. The cold war will end when Moscow judges it better to accept a truly free inspection system and international armaments control—at the cost of the Iron Curtain and the foreseeable end of Russian Communism—rather than persist in an increasingly expensive and fruitless arms race; and when Peking judges it better to accept a radical change in agricultural policy—at the cost of the virtual end of Chinese Communism—rather than to strain and starve further in an increasingly expensive and fruitless effort to expand Chinese Communist power in vain.

2. The time horizon for these climactic decisions cannot be predicted with precision; but they are about as clear as any such predictions are likely to be in the full confusion of historical circumstance. Give Moscow three to five years it needs to try and catch up in the arms race; prevent it from catching up in fact by maintaining, if possible, our net delivery advantage, and certainly by ruling out attack through a first-class air defense for the U.S. and Western Europe; give it not more and probably less than five further years for straining at great internal cost in food, light industry, housing, transport, etc., and then the latent forces for radical change will win, aided by the fact that Stalin's boys will then be out of the picture. Give Peking its first two five year plans (that is, to 1962–1964); frustrate its efforts at geographical expansion whether undertaken by soft means or hard; outrace its economic efforts in India, Burma, etc.; put Japan firmly on its feet within the Free World; and then the latent forces for radical change in Peking will win, aided by the fact that the Long March veterans will then be out of the picture.

3. This requires no U.S. action that is outside our orbit of freedom to move. It requires that at the key points of competition— notably the arms race and Asian economic growth—we throw our full weight in resources and technical know-how into the scales and make the enemy break his back in the effort to stay in the race.

4. There is not the slightest doubt in my mind that we have the basic resources to do this without affecting significantly the American standard of welfare; but neither can it be done on the cheap. It demands two things:

a. Our political leaders must go to the country, explain the dangers and explain the potentialities.

b. Our political leaders must ask for an enlarged and sustained effort, including more economic resources.

I understand full well the desire of both of our political parties to avoid charges of war-monger and spendthrift: for the Republicans to present themselves in 1956 as the party of peace and lowered taxes, for the Democrats to hope something except the real issue will turn up and get them back in power. But we must be clear that the enemy is using this time in Russia to catch up with us in the arms race, in China to outstrip in industrial power and military potential the rest of Asia. The arms race and economic development are problems in investment: investment takes time; if we slack off now in the face of our hungry, ardent enemy, we fall behind, losing that irretrievable asset time.

We are in a situation like the old school-yard sport of Indian wrestling where clean-cut victory goes to the one who holds out, under full pressure, that extra second. I am not talking about pressure in the aggressive or bombastic sense, but pressure in the form of making Moscow and Peking strain more and more to stay in the competitive cold war race.

I understand something else, too—the legitimate doubts about the exact position of our enemy. I have been, on and off, a professional intelligence officer for fourteen years, since the late summer of 1941. I know that intelligence is a problem in assessing a spectrum of possibilities; acting on intelligence is a problem in risk-taking, like banking, marriage, or other essential acts of life. One can make a series of assumptions about the enemy's position and conclude that we can come out of this all right without the kind of effort I propose (and which the Quantico group suggested). But it is risky banking, in which you assume that everything will break your way. It is not the way to play the risks when the stake is the survival of American society.

I have not the slightest doubt that the American people would respond to the challenge and possibilities of winning the cold war, if the choices were defined, and the requisite effort suggested. They cannot do it blind.

I urge upon you, then, and upon the others who alone know the facts and bear the constitutional responsibility of executive leadership that it may now be the time to evoke the energies, talents and resources of the American people at a new level, whose goal is peaceful victory.

Set this letter aside now. Perhaps Geneva will reveal that my timing is off and we can proceed directly and seriously to peace. But read it again if what we see is merely a clever playing for time, an effort to disrupt the unity and to diminish the effort of the West with gestures and blandishments. For then it will be the time to say to the American people that at the highest level we found no se-rious intent to end the arms race; and that the protection of our society requires a higher level of effort or sacrifice.

Yours,

W. W. Rostow

P.S. I enclose, as promised, a rough draft of a possible opening statement at Geneva which Max Millikan and I worked up, plus a memorandum explaining the considerations which entered into its construction.

Appendix H

Jackson's Account of Dinner with Dulles on the Eve of His Departure for Geneva and Dulles' Response

[*Note:* This appendix contains C. D. Jackson's contemporary account of a rather remarkable presummit dinner conversation with Dulles as well as Dulles' response of July 25. (The account of the dinner conversation is from the C. D. Jackson Papers, box 56, "Log-1955" folder, Dwight D. Eisenhower Library; the letter from Dulles is from the John Foster Dulles Papers, Correspondence Series, box 94, C. D. Jackson folder, Princeton University Library.)]

Monday, July 11, 1955

Dinner with Foster and Janet Dulles—36 hours before he left for Geneva. After dinner Mrs. Dulles left, and Foster unburdened, as expected, because invitation to dinner had been on basis of "alone so we can talk about things."

His opening gambit was, "I am terribly worried about this Geneva Conference". I asked for causes of worry. He said: "I have two major causes. First is that I am deathly afraid our allies might not come up to scratch. The French are so uncertain, so unhappy, and in such a mess all over everywhere that they may fall for some Soviet trick which would give France the illusion of being protected against a rearmed Germany.

"Eden is still in love with the idea of an Eden Plan for Germany. You remember in Berlin in '54 it was an accident of the seating arrangement that made our agreed-upon proposal for the unification of Germany be spoken by Eden, at which time it became labeled 'Eden Plan'. In his case I am very much afraid that he may accept some near disastrous compromise in order to have whatever it is labeled 'Eden Plan'.

"But what I am most worried about is the President. He and I have a relationship, both personal and operating, that has rarely existed between a Secretary of State and his President. As you know, I have nothing but admiration and respect for him, both as a person and as a man aware of foreign policy and conference pitfalls. Yet he is so inclined to be humanly generous, to accept a superficial tactical smile as evidence of inner warmth, that he might in a personal moment with the Russians accept a promise or a proposition at face value and upset the apple cart. Don't forget that informal buffet dinners will be the regular procedure every day, at which time I estimate the real work will be done, and it is at that time that I am particularly afraid that the Russians may get in their 'real work' with the President.

"We have come such a long way by being firm, occasionally disagreeably firm, that I would hate to see the whole edifice undermined in response to a smile.

"As I was saying to the Senate Committee which leaked my phrase about the possibility of Soviet collapse, we are in the situation of being prepared to run a mile in competition with another runner whose distance suddenly appears to be a quarter mile. At the quarter mile mark, the Russian quarter miler says to the American miler, 'This is really a quarter mile race, you know, and why don't we call it off now?'

"The President likes things to be right, and pleasant, between people. He tires when an unpleasantness is dragged out indefinitely. For instance, on the Bricker Amendment—that brother of his in the Middle West, the reactionary one, I can't remember his name—got hold of the President the other day and gave him a long story about giving in on the Bricker Amendment. The President got hold of me and said that he was tired of the endless bickering and wrangling and unpleasantness, and since it didn't really amount to much anyway, why shouldn't we give in and accept some kind of compromise language and let Bricker have his amendment.

"I happened to think of some language in George Washington's Farewell Address, where he made some mention of the fact that only the pragmatic tests of time would tell whether or not the Constitution should be amended, and how, and he urged that no advance theoretical amending be done—and it so happens that since the beginning of our Constitution all Amendments have been as the result of actual experience and need.

"I told this to the President—told him that he would be the first President of the United States who had ever amended the Constitution on the basis of a theory as to the future—that for Bricker to be right it would require the conjunction of a President who gave something away internationally which was unconstitutional, and a Senate which would ratify that agreement, and a Supreme Court which would confirm. *If*, and I underscore if, all these three things happened, then the danger that Bricker is trying to forestall might exist, and that does not take into account the fact that the Congress could upset it if it wished to.

"The President was impressed, and told me the next day that he had read his brother the particular passage from George Washington.

"But you see what I mean. He was tiring of running the full mile on the Bricker Amendment."

At that point I interrupted to ask about the "imminent collapse" leak from the Senate Foreign Relations Committee closed hearing. Dulles replied that (a) it was an executive session and off the record, (b) he could not talk convincingly to these Hill committees unless he could talk freely, (c) "I was frankly laying it on thick. After all, I was trying to persuade these men that this was not the time to call off that mile race, just because the quarter miler was getting tired. I pointed out to them with all the vehemence that I could that we had reached this point consciously, expensively, and sometimes painfully, but that it had paid off. Furthermore, I emphasized and reemphasized that what Russia had predicted for our system—namely, collapse—was precisely what appeared to be about to happen to them. I don't recall using the adjective 'imminent', but I certainly elaborated on the deepening cracks in the Soviet political and economic structure."

After rambling around on various details, Dulles said: "You know, I may have to be the Devil at Geneva, and I dread the prospect."

This gave me my cue to jump in and throw the mile–quarter mile simile right back at him. It was not a question of being a devil, but running that full mile, which he had so successfully started.

I added that for the first time in many, many years the United States had a real Secretary of State, and furthermore had a real

Secretary of State as a close partner rather than a competitor of the President. I reminded him of the words and the warmth of tone that Eisenhower had used many times, most recently in San Francisco, referring to his "good friend and trusted adviser, the Secretary of State". That relationship had come about largely as a result of Foster's courage and wisdom. I reminded him of the flap over "agonizing reappraisal", and the worse than flap over his refusal to stop off in Paris en route to see Adenauer in Bonn after the defeat of EDC . . . reminded him of his intelligent generosity in throwing bouquet after bouquet to Eden during the development of the Paris Accords plan after the defeat of EDC. All these things he had been blamed for, and yet the passage of time had proved him absolutely right. If that meant being a devil, well, then, let him be a devil again at Geneva, but a devil with his chin up.

Dulles then went into a rather pathetic little rumination about columnists, who repeatedly had descended upon him like wolves and then 3−4−5 months later when he had been proved right, had never uttered a word of correction. I told him that he should not worry about this at all, or certainly not beyond the initial irritation of whatever it was they printed. After all, columnists are in the business of going out on a limb 1−2−3−4−5 times a week, and it is agin the nature of the human animal 3−4−5 months later to type out "Folks, I was wrong about that fellow Dulles."

Interspersed in all the above was reference to Trieste, for which Dulles took full credit as something he had wanted to do ever since he got his job. Also a very interesting reference to the heat that Eden turned on during the British campaign to get the U.S. to agree to the parley at the Summit. Dulles said that at one moment when he could hardly believe that it was as important as Eden was apparently making it, he got hold of Harold Macmillan and put the question bluntly to him in terms of "I am amazed at these repeated requests from Eden—will you please tell me straight whether this is simply one of a half dozen things the Conservatives have thought of which might be of help to them in the campaign, or whether this is really of utmost importance." Macmillan replied, "It is of the utmost importance; in fact, if we don't get it, we may very well lose the election". So Dulles agreed then and there.

Picking up from the "devil at Geneva" dialogue, Dulles then said, "To my mind this is much more serious than the way we have been discussing it. In fact, this is something that I have never breathed to a soul, or even intimated, and I suppose there is not anybody else I could actually say it to. My big problem is a personal problem. I am afraid that either something will go wrong in Geneva, some slip of the allies, some slip of the President's, which will put me in the position of having to go along with a kind of foreign policy for the U.S. which could be described as appeasement—no, appeasement is too strong a word, but you know what I mean—or, on the other hand, I may have to behave in such a way at Geneva that my usefulness as Secretary of State, both domestically and abroad, will come to an end."

This was said with a depth of emotion on his part such as I had never heard before, and I was quite rocked.

I thought it was time to really give him a fight talk, so I picked up all over again on the mile race, on the success of the Dulles foreign policy, on his relationship with the President, on the status of his stock vis à vis Eden, on the fact that the President was no bubble head, that sure, he might get a little over-cozy with Zhukov if Zhukov turned up at the conference (Dulles interrupted to say that although the Soviet Delegation had not yet been announced, he had heard that Zhukov would probably be a member of the delegation for the express purpose of softening up the President), that Dulles' stock in the U.S. was very high (Dulles interrupted glowingly, "Yes, the latest Gallup Poll puts approval of my policies at 65% "), that his stock with the man in the street abroad was probably considerably higher than he thought, and anyhow, what the hell had he done all these things for—for the greater glory of John Foster Dulles or for the United States of America?

It was quite corny and somewhat like a football coach between halves, but it seemed to work, because as I then had to leave, he took me to the door, grabbed me by both arms, and said, "I am so grateful to you for having come down".

I told him that I was grateful to him for having been taken so tremendously into his innermost confidence, and added that I thought I would send him an edelweiss, which as he knew, was the reward of courage in Switzerland.

Footnote to this is that I commissioned Laguerre to purchase some kind of edelweiss good luck charm in Geneva and send it to Foster with a note from me saying, "As you know, only the most steadfast and courageous climber gets his edelweiss. I am sending you this one *before* the climb because I know you will earn a whole bouquet."

July 25, 1955

Dear C.D.:

It gave me much cheer to receive at Geneva your edelweiss. I still do not dare to wear it as I await your verdict on the outcome.

Personally, I feel reasonably satisfied. You know how nervous I was. I think we have avoided the most dangerous pitfalls and came out with some pluses, of which the most conspicuous was the President's proposal on mutual aerial inspection.

Faithfully yours,
John Foster Dulles

This was dictated before I saw you.

The Honorable
  C.D. Jackson
    9 Rockefeller Place
      New York, New York

JFD:cjp

Appendix I

Jackson's Letters to Eisenhower and Dulles on the Quantico Report

[*Note:* C. D. Jackson, at Rockefeller's suggestion, wrote to Eisenhower and Dulles about the Quantico meeting in an effort to enlist their sympathetic interest—in the latter case without notable success. (The letter to Eisenhower is from the C. D. Jackson Papers, box 41, "Eisenhower Correspondence through 1956" folder 1; the letter to Dulles is from box 40, "John Foster Dulles" folder, Dwight D. Eisenhower Library.)]

June 13, 1955

Dear Mr. President:

Having just returned from Nelson Rockefeller's Quantico skull session, I wanted to send you this brief note to convey a personal reaction and a personal hope.

I think that the meeting was a great success, and its findings could be of enormous value. Nelson deserves high praise for having carried it through in the face of quite an array of raised eyebrows, if not worse. And the fact that this group, containing an alarmingly large number of Ph.D.'s, was able to reach a dynamic consensus at the end of five days of argument, was to a great extent due to the atmosphere which Nelson created.

Even though you will probably not have the time to work your way through the entire report and appendices, I do hope that you will be able to read the first section of the report, as it is the mood-setting section from which the possible action items flow.

Your Penn State speech was wonderful, and of course had an extra special throb for me.

With every conceivable wish for you in this momentous summer

of 1955, when for the first time victory and peace are both beginning to get into focus, I am

Sincerely yours,
The President   C. D. Jackson
The White House
Washington, D.C.

bc: Mr. Nelson Rockefeller

Dear Foster:

I have just returned from the very interesting and exhilarating
Quantico meeting set up by Nelson Rockefeller, and I wanted to
send you this note to express the hope that the document produced there will not get too automatic a brushoff in the tepees.

I can fully appreciate the instinctive irritation of a large number
of intelligent, conscientious, seven-day-a-week, fifty-two-weeks-a-
year professionals at what may appear to them to be a one-shot, off-
the-top-of-the-head effort by some ad hoc enthusiasts.

I think the effort was considerably better than that, and merits
your personal perusal—at least the opening "Report" section. In it
you will see what I believe is a development of your own beliefs,
and of many of the things you have yourself stated publicly as well
as privately—notably your extraordinary television report on your
return from the Austrian signing.

This summer may indeed be the Summer of Decision, because for
the first time we can begin to see the outlines of victory with peace
in diplomatic reality and beyond the confines of our own hope and
faith.

All we tried to do was to state the opportunity, generate a mood,
and toss into your hopper, for whatever you think they may be
worth, a few suggestions, without pride of either ownership or
authorship.

Strength to your arm.

All the best,
The Honorable John Foster Dulles   C. D. Jackson
The Secretary of State
Washington, D.C.

bc: Mr. Nelson Rockefeller

Appendix J

Dulles' Suggestions for Eisenhower's Presummit Talk to the American People

[*Note:* This transcript contains Dulles' verbal suggestions for Eisenhower's talk to the American people before his departure for Geneva. (From the John Foster Dulles Papers, Presidential Speech Series, box 3, "President's Opening Statement at Geneva" folder 1, Dwight D. Eisenhower Library.)]

7/13/55

Secretary Dulles' verbal suggestions for Friday TV

This is the first time any American President has gone abroad for a mission such as this, to deal with the Heads of other Governments to prevent future war—rather than to prosecute a war to victory, or immediately after a war.   unusual

You are obviously not taking this trip, which is not [unprecedented]* in American history, for other than a great purpose. What is the purpose? It is not primarily to find quick solutions—quickies don't work out in these matters. They prove to be disillusioning. They give a superficial interpretation, which leads to differences in the future. These complex problems can only be finally resolved by painstaking effort, thinking out of every detail—that is the stage that has to be right. But during these ten years that have ensued since the end of the Second World War, there have been many conferences that have tried to solve problems as merely technical things. They have all been just frustrations, struggles for power, propaganda battles—to pursue the problems that way is barren.

*Alteration made by J.F.D.

167

The purpose of this trip primarily is to see and help others, to generate new spirit, satisfy their longings and aspirations, demanding a way that should be sound, sparing them and their children the devastations of another war. The purpose is to see whether, out of yours and corresponding spirits, from the hearts of yours and other Heads of Government, there can't be generated first a new spirit and then a means of setting up working procedures for dealing with these problems other than the way it was done in the past.

If you can generate that spirit, it can be a great contribution to peace. That is why you are going. Don't expect out of this that detailed solution will come. Any solution found in 4 or 5 days would not be sound or stable. Fused into the process is spirit, which would be responsive to all humanity.

Peace means something more than just the absence of killing people. It is a state of mind where human aspiration can be realized. There are certain basic things without which you don't have peace. People must be permitted to associate together as they wish, organize the societies they want, form the type government they want—that is what America has always stood for—it is in our blood. That is the kind of peace we want.

Next Sunday you will be in Church in Geneva. We will all be praying together.

Appendix K

Two Presummit Speech Drafts Submitted to
Eisenhower by Rockefeller

[*Note:* These two speech drafts were submitted to Eisenhower by Rockefeller, forwarded a bit later to Dulles. The first is in the form of notes for a
predeparture speech to the American people; the second is a proposed
opening statement at the summit. The author contributed to the first and
drafted the second after discussions with Rockefeller, designing them in
ways which might move the U.S. toward the mutual inspection proposal.
(From the John Foster Dulles Papers, Presidential Speech Series, box 1,
"President's Opening Statement at Geneva" folder, Dwight D. Eisenhower
Library.)]

July 11, 1955

Dear Foster:

Attached is a copy of my memorandum to the President with the
drafts of two suggestions for his fifteen minute TV speech prior to
Geneva. I gave these to the President on Friday to take with him
over the weekend.

Sincerely,
Nelson A. Rockefeller
Special Assistant

The Honorable
The Secretary of State
Washington

MEMORANDUM FOR THE PRESIDENT

Attached are drafts of two suggestions for your fifteen minute TV speech prior to Geneva.

The first draft is a summary of developments since the war and a realistic appraisal of our hopes for the Big Four Conference. It attempts the attitude of dignity and firmness to which you referred. The second draft represents a warmer, more human approach, which contains much of the substance of the first.

I thought these might be helpful to you in your thinking about your speech this weekend.

Nelson A. Rockefeller

July 8, 1955

DRAFT OUTLINE OF THE PRESIDENT'S SPEECH
TO THE PEOPLE OF THE UNITED STATES

1. I am reporting to the People of the United States on the eve of departure for the Geneva Conference. I shall report again after my return.

   (a) This is in the American tradition of representative government.

   (b) I go not as an individual but as the responsible delegate of a free people—to interpret their will and aspirations before the nations represented at this meeting.

   (c) But the responsibility of national representatives in the forthcoming conference goes beyond any narrow interpretation of national power interests. No four men, and no four nations can, or should, attempt to speak for the people and nations of the world. And yet, the lives of everyone in the world today, and for generations to come, may be affected profoundly by whether or not those at this meeting are able to resolve existing differences. The awesome developments in the arts of destruction make it imperative that each of us shall view national interests in their relationship to the interest of all mankind.

   (d) Too many people have given their lives, have suffered untold anguish and privation, have sacrificed their comfort and their treasure in the hope of achieving security and freedom, to make tenable a rigid unwillingness to explore any avenue through which these ends might be won. We cannot shirk any effort, however arduous, that promises to contribute. It is in this spirit that I shall be representing you at Geneva.

2. The United States has no interests to serve that cannot be freely aired in any forum of the world.

(a) We are irrevocably determined to preserve our own fabric of political, social and economic institutions and values—a fabric that incorporates a maximum of freedom for evolutionary change—but we do not seek to impose our institutions upon others who elect to follow different patterns.

(b) We are determined to maintain whatever level of armed strength is required for our security, but we are solemnly pledged never to employ it for aggression. We shall always and gladly be prepared to reduce it by any degree that the limits of safety permit.

(c) We are committed to a variety of security engagements with other friendly nations. These engagements are mutually binding solely for purposes of defense against aggression. They contain no commitment for aid in wars that might arise from the aggressive acts of any of the contracting parties. Again we will always be willing to scale down the level of jointly maintained defensive forces to the minimum dictated by common security requirements.

(d) We deeply cherish the system that has provided us with a growth economy that has yielded a high and progressively improving living level to all citizens of the United States, but this is not a threat to the economic advancement of other nations. On the contrary, we are so firmly convinced that vigorously thriving economies throughout the world are not only humanly but economically desirable that we have provided billions of dollars in each of the past ten years to assist other nations in the task of economic reconstruction and development. Despite the heavy burden of current armament expenditures, we are planning to increase the outlays for economic assistance to the underdeveloped areas of the world in the current fiscal year.

Unilaterally we have taken important steps to open to them and other nations knowledge and facilities that will permit them to share in the tremendous promise of peaceful applications of atomic energy. We have invited—and we shall repeat the invitation at Geneva—the nations of the world to join with us in pledging to commit a substantial percentage of whatever savings it may be possible to effect through agreed-upon scale down of armaments to the task of helping to bring about true growth economies in the underdeveloped areas.

3. The interests of the United States hold no threat to any nation unless our steadfast determination to protect ourselves and other friendly nations against aggression be interpreted as a threat.

(a) At the end of World War II, this country accepted in good faith the concept that the major powers could reach agreement upon the great security issues of the world under the machinery of negotiation provided in the United Nations. Unilaterally we dismantled our armed forces and promptly proposed a program for international control of atomic weapons.

(b) The latter proposal was rejected, and the period of Western military impotency witnessed in Europe alone the military, political, social and economic domination of Bulgaria, Rumania, Poland, Czechoslovakia, Hungary, Albania and Eastern Germany by the fully armed Soviet power. Where Soviet military encroachment halted, we have seen an unrelenting campaign of subversion and intimidation throughout the world that continues to the present day.

(c) It is this sustained Soviet campaign, and similar encroachments by China in the Far East under the umbrella of Soviet alliance, that have split the world. The military strength that has been built in the Free World was our reluctantly adopted answer to these challenges. It has no other purpose than the provision of defense against progressive engulfment. We are more than willing to embrace and to help create any opportunity that promises to provide genuine security through other and better means than an armaments race that robs all peoples of the standards of human welfare that are within their grasp.

4. It is our fervent hope that the Soviet representatives have come to this conference seriously prepared to explore different and more constructive ways of conducting international affairs than those which have characterized Soviet action in the last ten years.

(a) They have asserted that their present purposes are peaceful and explained their concentrated emphasis on military build-up as defensive. It is hard for us to understand how they could have so seriously misinterpreted our motives as to believe that our own defensive efforts threatened legitimate Russian national interests in any way. But if these are indeed the true aims of the present Soviet leaders, the prospects for results from the conference are good.

(b) In this event they, like us, have powerful reasons for finding an insurance of security in some form other than an arms race. They must in this event be eager to apply the fruits of their economic progress to increasing the well being and standards of living of their people. They have up to now been unable to devote any significant fraction of their energies to this constructive task because of the concentration of their economy on weapons and instruments of war and the heavy industry to support them. If they are now seriously seeking ways of freeing their economic, intellectual, and spiritual resources from the heavy demands of a garrison state for the purposes of constructive development our talks can make progress. In this event we are confident that, step by step and with patience, we can in time, find a basis for security on which both we and they can fully rely without continuation of the arms race.

(c) If on the other hand their intentions are not defensive but remain aggressive, and if the purpose of the current phase of their policy is to lull us into a relaxation they can later exploit, the conference will produce no useful results, and they will fail in their objectives. We have earned our status as veterans of the cold war and we shall not mistake the shadow for the substance. We are determined to explore their intentions seriously and soberly. We are prepared to meet good faith more than half way, but for their sake as well as ours we hope they really mean what they have been saying recently.

5. You may be assured that in this initial conference we shall do our utmost to see that all issues that are importantly contributing to tensions on either side are laid upon the table for frank discussion.

   (a) Among the most important of these are certainly the control of armaments, agreement upon the status of a unified Germany in Europe; similar problems with respect to the once independent countries of Eastern Europe; the problem of the use of subversion in all of its diverse forms across national boundaries; and that of the opening up of areas now sealed off from access to the free flow of ideas, communications, travel and trade.

   (b) Upon all of these issues, and upon others, the United States is prepared to make its positions clear in terms honestly designed to explore possibilities for their resolution rather than to score propaganda victories.

   (c) But you must be clear in your understanding that such issues cannot be settled in the brief discussions in Geneva. The most that can be hoped for is that divergencies in viewpoint will be clarified, and the ground work laid for the painstaking working out of accommodations under appropriate auspices. There is more than the time factor involved. All of the issues involve nations that will not be represented in the Geneva conversations, and the day has passed when a few nations possessed of the largest battalions can control the destinies of others without consultation. The United States would be unwilling to participate in such dispositions even if it were practicable to do so.

6. While time and broad consultation with all parties at interest are indispensable elements to the goal of relaxing world tensions, it should be possible to take some preliminary forward steps with relative promptness.

   (a) Confidence is basic to the relaxation of tensions, and confidence is an element that is effectually halted by curtains, whatever their composition. Before peoples can trust one another, they must learn to know one another.

(b) I am confident that no proposal for the reduction of armaments or military systems can make headway until a system for mutual inspection has been established and proved effective in operation to the satisfaction of both parties. In my judgment this is an essential prerequisite to any armament limitation agreement. The acceptance of this principle will serve as a test of the sincerity of suggestions offered in this field.

(c) Similarly, I believe that a willingness to allow a much wider latitude to the flow of ideas and a much freer exchange of personal contacts should be given high precedence in the time table of accommodations that are to be negotiated. I cannot escape the feeling that barriers between peoples are active breeders of distrust. And again I feel that the dispositions to promote progress along these lines will serve as an index of the good faith behind other proposals for lessening tensions.

7. Although the conference in Geneva will be concerned largely with problems relating to armament control and to European matters, I want to refer back to my earlier remark about peoples who will not be represented.

(a) In Asia, in the Middle East, and in Africa powerful new aspirations for independence, human dignity, and economic progress are not merely present but beginning to produce heartening results. Like all great revolutionary changes the coming of the less developed parts of the world to independence and responsibility is not necessarily a smooth process. It presents many difficult problems for us all. But it is a heartening spectacle, which the American government and the American people view with hope and even excitement. We are engaged around the world in many acts of partnership with the peoples of these new nations.

(b) Meanwhile, in Latin America similar developments, somewhat more advanced, are going on; and the policy of Free World partnership goes forward.

(c) We who are to meet at Geneva will be gravely in error if we do not recognize the enormous changes of the past decade. When the war ended the Big Three represented virtually the only effective sources of power and influence in the world. This is no longer the case. Power and influence have spread in many directions. Men in many nations have taken the measure of the world in which they find themselves; and they are asserting with conviction and confidence the policies they wish to see followed within their nations and on the world scene. I am sure that the second half of this century will not go down in history as the age of satellite states.

(d) The great powers of the world cannot hold positions of leadership and influence merely because they possess and can manufacture weapons of mass destruction. As for the United States, we know that our influence depends now and will depend increasingly on whether we are an effective force for peace, for material progress, for the free interchange of ideas on which spiritual progress must rest, and, above all, for national independence and human dignity.

Because of our history and our deepest tradition Americans can only welcome this diffusion of power and influence, based as it is on the acceptance of ideals and ambitions so close to our own. So long as these trends develop freely, in free nations, we have no fear for the place of America in the world.

(e) These developments bear directly on the meetings I shall attend in Geneva. The peoples of the world are impatient—and properly so—that the major powers find ways of protecting their own security which do not split nations and continents, which do not waste the world's resources and make men fearful for themselves and their children. Accordingly, as I have mentioned, I shall renew at Geneva my suggestion that some substantial percentage of any savings resulting from armament reduction should be pledged to the constructive purpose of assisting economic development where needed.

8. Finally, I will say this:
   (a) Until the very day that alternative measures we can trust are in effect, we of the Free World must persist in our efforts to protect our societies and to strengthen the collective arrangements we have painstakingly built.
   (b) We shall abandon no element in our present security arrangements unless we are assured that the next step will increase and not diminish the security of the Free World. We shall not mistake words for deeds. But we shall keep in our minds and our hearts a bold vision of the substance of peace; and we shall work with patience and ardor to make it a reality.
   (c) I should feel strengthened if I could feel that your prayers were added to my own that I may report upon the higher rather than the lower key on my return.

SUMMIT SPEECH
W. W. Rostow
June 20, 1955

DRAFT OF PROPOSED PRESIDENTIAL STATEMENT

The United States comes to these meetings determined to answer a simple question: is it possible now seriously to move toward peace, in Europe and in the world? We come prepared with positive and constructive proposals to this end, which my colleagues and I will lay on the table in the course of these conferences.

In order to understand the spirit and purpose of the American position, it is necessary to recall frankly what our common experience has been since the end of the Second World War.

In 1945 the United States accepted in good faith the concept that the major powers would find agreement by negotiation on the great security questions of the world leaving to each nation the right to determine its own form of political, social, and economic organization. Acting on the assumption that this form of world organization would prove workable the United States unilaterally dismantled its armed forces and promptly proposed a scheme for international control of atomic weapons.

The Soviet reply to the American position was simple and clear. Stalin judged the United States to be acting from weakness and he proceeded to exploit that weakness. Our proposals for the control of atomic weapons were rejected and a frightful arms race was launched. Simultaneously Stalin launched a world-wide campaign to expand Soviet power by imposing on new areas Soviet forms of political, social, and economic organization, and Soviet military power. The list in Europe alone is long and we should not forget it: Bulgaria, Rumania, Poland, Czechoslovakia, Hungary, Albania, and Eastern Germany. Where Soviet victory could not be achieved we have seen an unrelenting campaign of subversion and intimidation throughout the world which goes on to the present day.

It is this sustained Soviet campaign which has split the world, bringing us time after time to the brink of general war, denying the peoples of Russia as well as the rest of the world the security they seek and the standards of human welfare that are within their grasp.

Slowly, reluctantly the peoples of the Free World recognized the nature of the threat and accepted the challenge. We have maintained our position in the arms race and built in Europe a unified structure for military defense. We have together rebuilt the damage of war and given our economies a momentum lacking in the Western world since 1914. We come here to meet the Soviet chief of state, eager for peace, but clear in our minds as to what the foundations for peace must be. We are veterans of the cold war and we shall not mistake the shadow for the substance.

It is our fervent hope that the Soviet representatives have come to this conference seriously prepared to explore different and more constructive ways of conducting international affairs than those which have characterized Soviet action in the last ten years. They have asserted that their present purposes are peaceful and explained their concentrated emphasis on military build-up as defensive. It is hard for us to understand how they could have so seriously misinterpreted our motives as to believe that our own defensive efforts threatened legitimate Russian national interests in any way. But if these are indeed the true motives of the present Soviet leaders, the prospects for results from the conference are good.

In this event they, like us, have powerful reasons for finding an insurance of security in some form other than an arms race. They must in this event be eager to apply the fruits of their economic progress to increasing the well being and standards of living of their people. They have up to now been unable to devote any significant fraction of their energies to this constructive task because of the concentration of their economy on weapons and instruments of war and the heavy industry to support them. If they are now seriously seeking ways of freeing their economic, intellectual, and spiritual resources from the heavy demands of a garrison state for the purposes of constructive development our talks can make progress. In this event we are confident that, step by step and with patience, we can in time, find a basis for security on which both we and they can fully rely without continuation of the arms race.

If on the other hand their intentions are not defensive but remain aggressive, and if the purpose of the current phase of their policy is to lull us into a relaxation they can later exploit, the conference will produce no useful results, and they will fail in their objective. We are determined to explore their intentions seriously and soberly. We are prepared for any outcome, but for their sake as well as ours we hope they really mean what they have been saying recently.

What then is the substance of our task?

We face in this European Conference two overriding issues: the control of armaments; and the future of Germany in Europe.

No system of controlled armaments can provide security unless it is backed by extensive and thorough measures of mutual inspection. Such measures can never wholly eliminate the risk of sudden attack, but we believe they would make the risk very low. Can such measures be reconciled with the freedom of nations to pursue their own political and economic life? With modern weapons this reconciliation is not easy. We believe that it is possible; and we shall lay before the forthcoming conference specific measures to this end. We shall await with interest and attention the Soviet reaction to these proposals.

And now, what of Germany? There Russia has clung to its postwar zone of occupation creating by force a political and economic system in the image of the Soviet Union.

Here the substance of the matter is whether or not the Soviet Union is prepared to join with us in insuring genuinely free elections throughout all of Germany.

Let me repeat, I see no possibility of moving seriously toward the ending of the arms race until it is demonstrated as a matter of fact that an effective inspection system, which we all can trust, will actually work. This is the place to begin on the control of armaments; and we will make precise proposals to this effect. I see no possibility of moving seriously on the question of Germany until it is demonstrated as a matter of fact that free German elections can take place throughout all of Germany; and we will make precise proposals on this point as well.

Both with respect to the control of armaments and with respect to the freeing of Germany the larger question is this: can we begin concretely and practically to create the underlying conditions for peace? This must include a much wider exchange of ideas, a much freer exchange of personal contacts, and higher levels of trade. In addition to our central proposals on the control of armaments and on Germany, we are anxious to explore on a practical basis measures of this kind.

Although we must begin with practical steps, building step by step a true and firm foundation for peace, it is essential that we not lose sight of where we want to go.

Our first goal must be a world from which there has been lifted the fear of war and the costs of the arms race. There is no substitute for an effective system of arms control.

But let me state a warning. Let us assume that the best happens. Let us assume that we move toward an effective system of armaments control, with satisfactory measures for mutual inspection. Such a system can never permit any of us to relax. In the company of all other nations, large and small, who share our interest in the control of armaments, the United States will maintain eternal vigilance in enforcing its provisions. Under no foreseeable circumstances will the United States turn in on itself and leave its security in other hands.

What is our ultimate goal in Germany? We must begin by demonstrating that free elections can be held throughout Germany; but this is the beginning not the end of the task. Germany is now split;

and all Germans must look forward impatiently to the day when their nation is again unified.

More than that, Europe itself is split. From Warsaw to Paris, from Budapest to Brussels, Europeans know in their hearts that there will be no real peace and security in the world until the nations and peoples of Europe can move and trade and exchange freely the ideas which are the product of a common culture, over the length and breadth of this great Continent. This demands that every nation in Europe be free to create its own form of political and economic organization, as indeed, the unimplemented but still valid wartime agreements of the allies specifically require.

Germany reunited would be a large and powerful country. But it would, like other countries, be subject to collective measures of armaments control. And I am confident on the basis of the experience of Western Europe since 1947 that the method of economic and political cooperation can be further developed so that the European nations, large and small, can actively share as equals in the common enterprises of Europe. More than that I sense that the people of Germany know that their destiny lies in making a maximum constructive contribution to the emergence of a peaceful, productive, and increasingly united Continent.

Although this conference is concerned primarily with the problem of the control of armaments and with Europe we must not forget the worldwide setting in which we meet.

In Asia, in the Middle East, and in Africa powerful new aspirations for independence, human dignity, and economic progress are not merely present but beginning to produce heartening results. Like all great revolutionary changes the coming of the less developed parts of the world to independence and responsibility is not necessarily a smooth process. It presents many difficult problems for us all. But it is a heartening spectacle, which the American government and the American people view with hope and even excitement. We are engaged around the world in many acts of partnership with the peoples of these new nations.

Meanwhile, in Latin America similar developments, somewhat more advanced, are going on; and the policy of Free World partnership goes forward.

We around this table will be gravely in error if we do not recognize the enormous changes of the past decade. When the war ended the Big Three represented virtually the only effective sources of power and influence in the world. This is no longer the case. Power and influence have spread in many directions. Men in many nations have taken the measure of the world in which they find themselves; and they are asserting with conviction and confidence the policies they wish to see followed within their nations and on the world scene. I am sure that the second half of this century will not go down in history as the age of satellite states.

The great powers of the world cannot hold positions of leadership and influence merely because they possess and can manufacture weapons of mass destruction. As for the United States, we know that our influence depends now and will depend increasingly on whether we are an effective force for peace, for material progress, for the free interchange of ideas on which spiritual progress must rest, and, above all, for national independence and human dignity.

Because of our history and our deepest tradition Americans can only welcome this diffusion of power and influence, based as it is on the acceptance of ideals and ambitions so close to our own. So long as these trends develop freely, in free nations, we have no fear for the place of America in the world.

These developments bear directly on our meetings here in Geneva. We must never forget that our possession of modern weapons of mass destruction and our legal obligation to negotiate concerning the future of Germany arising from the war are a grave responsibility. The peoples of the world are impatient—and properly so— that the major powers find ways of protecting their own security which do not split nations and continents, which do not waste the world's resources and make men fearful for themselves and for their children.

I proposed two years ago that a portion of our savings from disarmament be made available for accelerating the economic development of the growing new nations of the world. Despite the continued costs of the armaments race we are even now increasing the resources available for this purpose from the United States. I should like to repeat what I said in April 1953:

> This Government is ready to ask its people to join with all nations in devoting a substantial percentage of the savings

achieved by disarmament to a fund for world aid and reconstruction. The purposes of this great work would be to help other peoples to develop the undeveloped areas of the world, to stimulate profitable and fair world trade, to assist all peoples to know the blessings of productive freedom.

I shall propose that other nations join in this pledge.

Until the very day that alternative measures we can trust are in effect, we of the Free World must persist in our efforts to protect our societies and to strengthen the collective arrangements we have painstakingly built.

We shall abandon no element in our present security arrangements unless we are assured that the next step will increase and not diminish the security of the Free World. We shall not mistake words for deeds. But we shall keep in our minds and our hearts a bold vision of the substance of peace; and we shall work with patience and ardor to make it a reality.

Appendix L

Postsummit Stassen Letter to Rockefeller

[*Note:* Stassen's postsummit letter graciously acknowledges Rockefeller's role in the Open Skies initiative, notably the text transmitted from Paris to Geneva on July 19. (From papers personally released for publication by Nelson Rockefeller.)]

July 27, 1955

Dear Nelson:

Since your memorandum in Paris played such an important part in what everyone now recognizes to have been a sound initiative at Geneva, I thought you might like to have the original back, particularly as its final paragraph on the quest for peace became a part of an historic document.

It was a great pleasure to work with you, and I look forward to our future association under the leadership of President Eisenhower which we both feel has come through at Geneva on a world basis in a manner similar to his earlier attainment of summit status in the United States.

Sincerely yours,

Harold E. Stassen

Enclosure

Appendix M

State Department Position Papers on the Summit

[*Note:* This appendix includes State Department estimates of prospects for the U.S. and the U.S.S.R. achieving their respective objectives at the summit, after Dulles' personal editing. (From the Dwight D. Eisenhower Papers, Ann Whitman Files, International Meetings Series, box 1, "Geneva Conference, July 18–23, 1955" folder 1, Dwight D. Eisenhower Library.)]

Paper III
ESTIMATE OF PROSPECT OF US ACHIEVING
ITS GOALS

1. (Unification of Germany) It will probably be possible to have this topic remitted to a future Four Power Foreign Ministers' meeting with participation of the Federal Republic through the Western powers and of GDR through the USSR. However, the Soviets will probably want to go slowly on this, and may use their invitation to Adenauer as a tactic of delay. Also, the progress here suggested depends upon progress under Item 2.

2. (European security—See also Soviet Item 6) It will probably be possible to get agreement that, concurrently with study of German unification, there will be negotiations between a group representing the NATO powers and a group representing the Warsaw powers designed to achieve a degree of demilitarization in Central Europe, and a level of European forces, within the context of which German unification might take place. Care must be taken lest this arrangement operate in effect to accept and consolidate the Soviet control over the satellites.

3. (Global level of armament) It will probably be possible to have the present UN Disarmament Subcommittee (Canada, France, UK, USSR and US) continue as the nucleus for discussion. It will be difficult, but not impossible, to have Big Four delegates instructed to concentrate in the first instance upon the machinery of supervision. It will probably not be possible or even desirable to exclude the concept of a world disarmament conference *after* sufficient progress has been made during the initial phase above described.

4. (Liberation of satellites) It will be difficult to get any formal undertaking from the Soviet Union with reference to the topic or even their acceptance of it as a proper topic for discussion. However, they may in fact move in that direction if we impress the Soviets deeply with the importance which the United States attaches to this subject and with the fact that we shall watch vigilantly to see what the developments are and use that as a rod for measuring the degree of cooperation which we can extend to the Soviet Union in other respects. After all, what we ask for is less than what the Soviets gave Tito.

5. (International Communism) Best progress may be made privately, as suggested above with reference to the satellites. However, preliminary talks with Molotov indicate that the Soviets may be willing at least to discuss this topic and perhaps to agree to go through certain motions, as ending the Cominform. A Soviet statement, as in the Bulganin-Tito communique, may be possible. But real progress will have to be judged by what happens, not by what is said.

6. (Ideas across the Iron Curtain) Probably some progress could be made here, although it may be conditioned upon reciprocal agreements to eliminate radio broadcasts, balloon flights and the like into the Soviet area. The net value of any possible reciprocal agreement would have to be carefully appraised.

7. (Atoms for peace) It is possible that if pressed the Soviets might be willing to agree to put up some small amount of fissionable material for this plan. The value of this result to the United States is chiefly psychological in seeming to have "put across" a plan much of the free world identifies with President Eisenhower.

Paper IV
ESTIMATE OF PROSPECT OF SOVIET UNION ACHIEVING
ITS GOALS

1. (Moral and social equality) The Soviets will probably make considerable gains in this respect. These gains can be minimized by the President avoiding social meetings where he will be photographed with Bulganin, Kruschev, etc., and by maintaining an austere countenance on occasions where photographing together is inevitable. Also, the extent of Soviet gain could be limited by public knowledge that the occasion was being used by the US to push for satellite liberation and liquidation of International Communism. Here we run into a conflict between a desire not to make the meeting into a propaganda forum and the fact that unless our position on these two topics is known, the Soviets will automatically gain very considerable advantage under this heading.

2. (Western relaxing) Unless the conference ends on a note of open discord, the Soviets will probably gain a considerable degree of relaxing on the part of the West, particularly in terms of NATO level of forces and German rearmament.

3. ("Ban the Bomb") It will probably be possible to prevent appreciable Soviet gains under this item by achieving the US goal 3.

4. (Trade) Again, unless the conference ends on a note of open discord, the result will probably be to ease gradually the scope of control now exerted by the Cocom Committee.

5. (Statement of principles) It will be possible to prevent any statement of principles lending itself to Communist propaganda either through (a) opposing any statement whatever or (b) having a statement of our own which avoids the Communist "clichés" which, although unobjectionable on their face, portray Communist origin.

In this connection, see JFD speech at San Francisco where he opposed Molotov's "seven principles" by saying that only one principle is needed, that is live up to the spirit of the UN Charter.

6. (All-Europe security system) It will be possible to prevent acceptance in principle of any plan which would tend to eliminate US presence from Europe. The outcome of this discussion could be as indicated in the discussion of Item 2 of US goals.

7. (Great power status to Communist China) It will be possible

to prevent any agreement on a Far Eastern conference, including Communist China and excluding the CHINATS. However, the United States cannot safely take a purely negative position in relation to this area where obviously tension is most acute. Probably the best solution is for the US to have some direct talks with the Chinese Communists which will slightly increase the scope and the level of the talks now being held at Geneva with reference to citizens of the two countries held by the other.

8. (US propaganda for war) By the very fact of bringing up this subject—if they do—the Soviets will gain some advantage. However, that can be minimized if we knock it down hard.

9. (Dividing the West) It will probably be impossible to prevent some slight increase within Germany of neutralism and demilitarization, and within France, of the public nostalgia for a resumption of special relations between France and Russia to contain Germany. However, if we handle our case right, this increase should not be substantial and it should be possible to offset it by a demonstration of the value to our three countries of standing together.

Notes

1. The physical setting of the meeting is evoked in Livingston Merchant's sixty-page "Recollections of the Summit Conference Geneva—1955," John Foster Dulles Papers, box 92, p. 37, Seeley G. Mudd Library, Princeton University. Merchant's account is a vivid portrait of what a summit conference entails for a senior staff officer. He concludes that the Open Skies proposal was "the most spectacular event of the Conference," "a sound concept," and "good propaganda"; but he does not deal with the origins or larger purposes of the proposal. He captures well, however, the authentic surprise and initial discomfiture of the Soviet delegation.

2. Dwight D. Eisenhower, *Mandate for Change, 1953–1956* (Garden City, N.Y.: Doubleday, 1963), pp. 521–522.

3. Responding to an earlier draft of this book, Paul Worthman provided me on May 15, 1981, with an invaluable and authoritative account of precisely where each of the three tech niques for photographing the Soviet Union stood as of the time of the Geneva summit. His role is made clear in what follows:

   Where We Stood in July 1955: Balloon Photo-Reconnaissance:

   The first study of the use of balloons for photo-reconnaissance was done by RAND Corporation in 1946 (at that time, RAND was a part of Douglas Aircraft). The development of polyethylene film as a new balloon fabric was fundamental in encouraging this study.

The idea was to fly balloons at a very high altitude (above known fighter capability), drifting them across the USSR, and recovering them over neutral or friendly territory. The use of polyethylene made it possible to fly the balloons at constant pressure-altitude (which means essentially at a pre-selected altitude). The Air Force had been experimenting with these balloons at Holloman Air Force Base, and, in the early 1950's, was using them to carry scientific equipment to high altitudes.

In the summer of 1951, while working at Air Force Headquarters, in the Pentagon, I wrote a directive to the Air Force Cambridge Research Center specifying a field program to study the very high altitude wind field. In 1940, the expression "high altitude" had meant above 10,000 feet; work with B-29's jumped the meaning to 25,000 feet. By 1950, 50,000 feet was a modern definition and it seemed to be a good idea to get some instruments at even higher altitudes: to get there, just for once, before the airplanes did. The directive required polyethylene balloons to be floated at staggered levels between 50,000 and 100,000 feet; the balloons would carry a transmitter which would enable one to locate them every two minutes. With launchings from three West Coast sites (Tillamook, Oregon; Vernalis, California; and Edwards Air Force Base, California), we believed we would get good coverage of the U.S. and that a typical crossing would take three days. The balloons used an automatic ballasting system whenever they needed to gain altitude. After about three days, they would descend to 28,000 feet, where a pressure-sensing cut-down device would take over. The balloon would float harmlessly to earth, the gondola would follow on a parachute, and the finder would receive a monetary reward for returning the gondola. We called this project MOBY DICK ("What a gleamy and dazzling thing, this splendid, great white whale!").

At the very time I was writing this directive, working in the Geophysics Branch, around the corner from my office another directive was being written by a friend in the Reconnaissance Branch. He was directing the Wright Air

Development Center to produce an operational plastic balloon for overflying the USSR. The 1946 RAND study would guide Wright Field's thinking. My friend and I believed these programs would complement each other quite nicely, with MOBY DICK furnishing important developmental technology to its operational counterpart (named WS-119L); it would also furnish a practically perfect "cover" for at least the developmental phase of WS-119L.

I was transferred to the Air Force Cambridge Research Center, to a staff position, in the Fall of 1951. Over the next two years, I was pleased to note the success of MOBY DICK, as hundreds of balloons swept across the United States at altitudes which helped deliver unique data to the Air Weather Service and the (then) U.S. Weather Bureau. Occasionally, to the delight of everyone in the program, a MOBY DICK balloon would make a very fast trip across the U.S., and sail out over the Atlantic, beeping away. Not to worry.

WS-119L was another story. The Wright Field engineers were not acquainted with polyethylene balloons and delegated that part of the development program to Holloman Air Force Base, retaining gondola development, camera development, and recovery work. They concentrated on the recovery problem, which appeared to be the most difficult; they were unable to solve it. The WS-119L specifications called for a capability to pick up a 600-lb gondola on the ground, on the water, and in the air. By early 1953, Wright Field technicians considered the project a disaster: one aircrew had almost crashed in field tests and no one had much stomach for carrying the work any farther.

A series of unusual circumstances led to my transfer from the Cambridge staff to a new laboratory—the Atmospheric Devices Laboratory—in the Spring of 1953. This lab, among other responsibilities, was given the job of MOBY DICK *and* WS-119L.

WS-119L had these basic technical problems, all requiring "instant" solution:

    a. How can one get polyethylene manufacturers to

make a very high quality film for the balloon program (no thin spots, please!), when all the big money is in seat covers and carrot-wrap?

b. How can one develop a gondola that will stay warm enough to protect our electronics and camera, when they are flying in the stratosphere for more than the usual three days?

c. How does one design a parachute capable of floating a 600-lb load safely from altitudes of 75–90,000 feet?

d. How does one recover a gondola safely in mid-air, say at 12–14,000 feet? (Water recovery and land pick-up looked solvable.)

Each of these problems was solved experimentally by August 1954. Production of equipment and crew-training were completed by August 1955. The flight program lasted from November 1955 to Spring 1956, producing, by the user's standards, excellent results. It was certainly the least expensive program that has ever been run on this specific problem.

There was some Soviet rhetoric (not very tough) over failed flights which dropped gondolas to earth prematurely. The reason for termination was never explained to us, but I later associated it with the fine progress Kelly Johnson was making at Lockheed's Skunk Works [where the U-2 was developed]. The very high altitude wind field weakens and shifts radically in the late Spring, so we knew we would not be flying, whatever the political situation, during summer months.

I did not see examples of the product until May 1961.

Although Gary Powers' trial, in 1960, was a serious affair, I could not help but smile at that part of the prosecution testimony in which G. Istomin, D. Sc. Tech., said that "The film is of a special grade designed for aerial surveys from high altitudes. Compared with the film used in American spy balloons of the 1956 model, the given grade has been improved . . ."

In 1957, the WS-119L camera (a beauty!) became the basis for the DISCOVERER satellite camera. Also, in 1957, the WS-119L mid-air recovery system was used—exactly as was—for outfitting the C-130's which were to recover satellite capsules in mid-air. By that time, I was stationed on the West Coast, in the Air Force Ballistic Missile Division, and shared responsibility for developing the DIS-COVERER program. We were all very grateful that there had once been a lighter-than Air Force.

Where We Stood in July 1955: U-2 Photo-Reconnaissance:

I did not participate in this program, but had a number of friends who did. The "Perry Dictum" was borne out when I asked one of the key persons when the first U-2 test flight was made and, after searching his memory, he missed it by a year. [The reference is to Robert Perry of RAND whose dictum is: "Don't give me your memories, give me your memoranda." I would modify the Perry Dictum only by saying a historian wants both, while maintaining, of course, a proper reserve about memories unsupported by documentary evidence.] The first test flight was made on August 6, 1955. The first overflight of the USSR was made in 1956. The USSR overflight program was curiously tentative; perhaps there was some feedback to President Eisenhower about which we do not know. The caution can be illustrated two ways, rather easily. If you plot all U-2 overflights of the USSR on a single map, the limitations of the effort are almost shocking. The second evidence is knowing that from early 1958 to April 1960, practically *no* overflights of the USSR were made (one uses the word "practically" because some of the overflights were so shallow as to scarcely qualify).

Where We Stood in July 1955: Satellite Photo-Reconnaissance:

In July 1955, we had no satellite photo-reconnaissance capability whatever. RAND had done a fine study of satellite reconnaissance in 1946; a second important set of studies was produced in 1952–3. There had been very limited development-testing of some sensor and read-out components. But the big problem—the unavailability of a booster—was simply insurmountable.

Recall that the first successful THOR did not fly until

December 19, 1957 and the first ATLAS success did not occur until August 29, 1958.

Satellite photo-reconnaissance came into its own August 18, 1960. (Please to ignore the persons who will insist it was August 10; they are wrong.)

4.   Paul Worthman commented as follows in a letter to me of May 15, 1981: "Very little work was being done on the satellite system in 1955. From 1955 through 1957, 'space' was literally a dirty word, not to be used by anyone in our government except NASA, and sparingly there. As late as 1957, (then) Major General B. A. Schriever had tough sledding getting $10 million for a satellite reconnaissance system and was *ordered* (hardly necessary, with that funding) to limit his effort to component development."

5.   Ibid. Paul Worthman comments: "I'll wager no one in our community *really knows* if this flight [KOSMOS I] produced intelligence information, but it is certainly the first flight in the series which we identify with Soviet satellite reconnaissance."

6.   This point is made by Stefan Possony in "Reconnaissance in Time Perspective," in Frederick J. Ossenbeck and Patricia C. Kroeck (eds.), *Open Space and Peace* (Stanford: Hoover Institution, 1964), pp. 30–31.

7.   Dwight D. Eisenhower, *Waging Peace, 1956–1961* (Garden City, N.Y.: Doubleday, 1965), p. 556.

8.   On this point Paul Worthman commented perceptively in his letter to me of May 15, 1981:

. . . one of the fastest fading recollections for the American public—and even the intelligence community—is the fact that the closed society was an extraordinarily effective device for the purposes of the Soviets. I see the open skies proposal in that context; it was one of a series of acts of near-desperation by our frustrated, worried national leaders. No one seems to remember *how* frustrated and *how* worried.

When one tells today's citizens that our leaders were deeply concerned about a surprise attack, or believed very sincerely that the probability of nuclear war was rather high, the listener shows nothing but disbelief. The listener has a great advantage: he knows how things turned out during that chapter—we were not attacked and we did not go to war.

9. *Khrushchev Remembers*, trans. and ed. by Strobe Talbott (Boston: Little, Brown, 1970), pp. 392–393.

10. *Khrushchev Remembers: The Last Testament*, trans. and ed. by Strobe Talbott (Boston: Little, Brown, 1974), pp. 374–375.

11. Marquis Childs adds another possible dimension to the reasons for Eisenhower's decision to go to Geneva (*Eisenhower: Captive Hero* [New York: Harcourt, Brace, 1958], pp. 205–206):

> There is some reason to believe that President Eisenhower's attitude toward the proposed summit meeting was different from that of his Secretary of State. By this time the Eisenhower reputation was sadly frayed. The image of the crusader had been blurred by the McCarthy madness and by the nagging, persistent futility of his efforts to bring his party together behind many important, constructive measures. The Democrats had won control over both houses of Congress in 1954. With the dimming of the Eisenhower luster, his critics were becoming bolder, although he still had a powerful hold on the country as hero, a folk figure larger than life-size, and a large proportion of the press continued to treat him with veneration, if not with awe. With his intuitive sense of drama and popular response, and with the precedents of 1942 and 1950, the meaning of a return to Europe in the role of peacemaker can scarcely have escaped him. The symbol of the hero-leader was in need of refurbishing. His mandate, out of the great electoral victory of 1952, had been to bring peace to the United States and the world. And so this new opportunity glowed against the murky horizon of the recent past with both a challenge and a promise.

12. Eisenhower details clearly the background to his decision to accept the summit meeting in his *Mandate for Change*, pp. 505–506.

13. Ibid., p. 508.

14. The individual supporting papers and their authors were:
    Tab 1—"Soviet Estimate of the Situation" (George Pettee)
    Tab 2—"The Requirements for U.S.-NATO to Win in the
        Arms Race with the USSR" with two annexes
        (Ellis Johnson)
    Tab 3—"Alliance and Coalition Problems"
        (a) "Does NATO Have a Position of Strength?"
            (Frederick S. Dunn)
        (b) "Asia Policy" (W. W. Rostow)
        (c) "Japan" (Paul Linebarger)
        (d) "Measures to Cope with Free-World Fears of
            the Bomb" (Stefan Possony)
        (e) "Air Defense of the United States and Western
            Europe" (Ellis Johnson)
        (f) "Factors Influencing the Morale of Allies"
            (George Pettee)
    Tab 4—"Straining the Sino-Soviet Alliance" with annex
        (Paul Linebarger)
    Tab 5—"An Institute for the Study of Peace" (George
        Pettee)
15. This interview was conducted by Hugh Morrow, of Rockefeller's staff, on July 14, 1977.
16. Dwight D. Eisenhower Papers, Ann Whitman Files, Whitman Diary Series, box 5, "Ann C. Whitman Diary, May 25, 1955" folder 2, Dwight D. Eisenhower Library.
17. John Foster Dulles Papers, Telephone Conversation Series, box 10, "White House Telephone Conversations, Mar.–Aug. 1955" folder 1, Dwight D. Eisenhower Library.
18. Dwight D. Eisenhower Papers, Ann Whitman Files, Whitman Diary Series, box 5, "Ann C. Whitman Diary, May 25, 1955" folder 2, Dwight D. Eisenhower Library.
19. Sherman Adams, *Firsthand Report* (New York: Harper, 1961), pp. 90–91.
20. Memorandum of telephone call from Sherman Adams, August 5, 1955, John Foster Dulles Papers, Telephone Conversation Series, box 10, "White House Telephone Conversations, Mar.–Aug. 1955" folder 1, Dwight D. Eisenhower Library.
21. Memorandum of conversation with the president, August 5, 1955, John Foster Dulles Papers, White House Memo Series,

box 3, "Meetings with the President—1955" folder 3, Dwight D. Eisenhower Library.

22. John Foster Dulles Papers, Telephone Conversation Series, box 10, "White House Telephone Conversations, Mar.–Aug. 1955" folder 1, Dwight D. Eisenhower Library.

23. Morrow interview.

24. John Foster Dulles Papers, Telephone Conversation Series, box 4, "Telephone Conversations, General, May–Aug. 1955" folder 6, Dwight D. Eisenhower Library.

25. Memorandum of telephone conversation with the president, July 6, 1955, John Foster Dulles Papers, Telephone Conversation Series, box 10, "White House Telephone Conversations, Mar.–Aug. 1955," Dwight D. Eisenhower Library.

26. Morrow interview.

27. Ibid.

28. Responding on May 4, 1981, to an earlier draft of this book, William Kintner recalled the meeting on July 18 as follows:

Nelson alone of our small group was sitting at the table. I was sitting directly behind him. After his initial presentation to Anderson, Radford, etc., the "Open Skies" proposal fell like a lead balloon. He turned around and asked, "What did I do?" And I said, "Do it again." It was at this time that Possony intervened and Radford finally got the idea—"I see what you fellows are doing—you are trying to open up the Soviet Union." Radford's observation won general acceptance of the group for the "Open Skies" proposal.

29. Reston's dispatch of July 20 undoubtedly reflected Dulles' background press conference of that day, given on a "not for attribution" basis, now available in the Dulles Papers at the Princeton University Library. The bulk of the briefing centered on whether progress could be made in reconciling Soviet proposals for an all-European security treaty with U.S., British, and French insistence that such a treaty must be accompanied by the emergence of a Germany unified on a democratic free election basis. The disarmament discussion scheduled for the next day was mentioned briefly several times in the course of Dulles' briefing. He noted, for example, that "there is more room for imaginative thinking" than on the

German problem, "which has been quite thoroughly hacked over for a period now of approximately eight years." On the arrival of Gruenther and Radford, about which he was questioned, in connection with the European security–German issue, Dulles said: "There is no possibility of discussing and exploring these problems just in the few hours these gentlemen will be here. We will give them a general overall picture of the way things are going. There has been a talk with them but it is not for the purpose of giving any technical studies to any of these proposals."

Dulles was asked bluntly: "Will the United States present any plan or proposal on disarmament?" He replied: "Well, we will follow the same practice with reference to disarmament that we have followed with reference to this matter [Germany]; namely, that we will indicate our broad philosophical approach. Indeed, that has already been done in the opening statement of the President, where he put special emphasis upon problems of inspection and viewing to prevent surprises. And there may be various illustrative things indicated by the various Ministers as to what might be done under that heading. But there again there will be nothing in the way of a concrete proposal of substance on a take-it-or-leave-it basis." In a further question on disarmament Dulles went no further than the relevant passage in Eisenhower's opening statement at Geneva.

When Dulles spoke to the press, Eisenhower had not yet indicated his firm decision to go ahead with Open Skies; and it would have been, in any case, inappropriate for Dulles to foreshadow it. But the background press conference makes quite clear why Reston and his colleagues were surprised on the next day when, indeed, "a concrete proposal of substance" was laid on the table by Eisenhower.

30. Log entry 1/16/54, C. D. Jackson Papers, box 56, "Log-1954" folder, Dwight D. Eisenhower Library.
31. Charles E. Bohlen, *Witness to History, 1929–1969* (New York: W. W. Norton, 1973), pp. 384–385. Bohlen was Eisenhower's personal interpreter at Geneva.
32. James Desmond, *Nelson Rockefeller: A Political Biography*

(New York: Macmillan, 1964), pp. 151–152. In the course of this study we sought and obtained declassification of the Quantico II report: "Psychological Aspects of United States Strategy," November 1955. It is to be found at the Eisenhower Library.

33. *International Security: The Military Aspect* (Garden City, N.Y.: Doubleday, 1958), pp. 62–64. The final text of the report of Panel II is to be found in *Prospect for America: The Rockefeller Panel Reports* (Garden City, N.Y.: Doubleday, 1958, 1959, 1960, 1961), pp. 93–155. The following are key passages:

It is the judgment of the panel that prepared this report that all is not well with present US security policies and operations. The over-all US strategic concept lags behind developments in technology and in the world political situation. Defense organization is unrelated in major ways to critically important military missions. Systems of budgets, appropriations, and financial management are out of gear with the radically accelerating flow of military developments. The United States system of alliances must be adapted to constantly changing strategic requirements. The United States is rapidly losing its lead in the race of military technology.

We are convinced that corrective steps must be taken now.

We believe that the security of the United States transcends normal budgetary considerations and that the national economy can afford the necessary measures.

In brief, the conclusions of the panel are:

I. The world knows that we would never fight a preventive war. But we and the rest of the free world must be prepared to resist any one of three types of aggression: all-out war, limited war, and non-overt aggression concealed as internal takeover by coup d'etat or by civil war.

II. In order to deter aggression, we must be prepared to fight a nuclear war either all-out or limited.

III. At present there are major shortcomings in our posture for both all-out war and limited war. Our retaliatory force is inadequately dispersed and protected. Our active and passive defense is insufficient. Moreover, we lack mobility and versatility for limited war.

IV. Basic changes in our defense organization are recommended to correct the inefficiency and duplication of effort growing out of interservice rivalry.

    a). The military departments should be removed from the channel of operational command.

    b). All of the operational military forces of the United States should be organized into unified commands to perform missions which are called for by our strategic requirements.

    c). The Chairman of the Joint Chiefs of Staff should be designated Principal Military Adviser to the Secretary of Defense and the President.

    d). The staff of the Joint Chiefs of Staff should be organized on a unified basis and placed under the control of the Chairman.

    e). All officers above the rank of Brigadier General or equivalent should receive their permanent promotions from the Department.

    f). The line of operational command should be from the President and the Secretary of Defense to the functional commanders through the Chairman of the Joint Chiefs of Staff in his capacity as Principal Military Adviser.

    g). The line of logistic command should be from the President through the Secretary of Defense to the Secretaries of the three military departments.

    h). The Secretary of Defense should be given authority over all research, development and procurement. He should have the right of cancellation and transfer of service programs together with their appropriations. He should also be given a direct appropriation for the conduct of research and development programs at the Defense Department level.

V. We must strengthen the regional groups of nations,

not as an alternative to the United Nations, but as its complement in line with Article 51 of the Charter.

VI. The United States must make a concerted effort to meet the joint security requirements of all partners in the alliances in which we participate by contributing to the development of a common strategic concept, by assisting in the re-equipping of allied forces by fostering political cohesiveness and by economic and technical cooperation.

VII. We must pool with our allies in NATO scientific and technical information, and provide them with nuclear weapons and delivery systems.

VIII. Civil defense must be part of our over-all strategic posture. A program must be undertaken to include a warning system and fall-out shelters.

IX. We must face the fact that a meaningful reduction of armaments must be preceded by a reduction of tensions and a settlement of outstanding issues that have divided the world since World War II. At the same time, concrete proposals to limit such wars as might be forced on us should be introduced into negotiations on reduction in forces. Even if the Soviet Union should reject our proposals, a unilateral declaration might be given a strong incentive to follow suit.

X. Starting immediately, defense expenditures must be increased substantially over the next few years. Testimony indicates that current deficiencies in our strategic position require additional expenditures each year of approximately $3 billion for the next several years. This does not include necessary increased appropriations for mutual assistance and for civil defense. Because we must maintain our present forces as we go into production on new weapons, such as missiles, the cost of military programs will continue to rise until at least 1965.

Specific recommendations include the following:

    a). Aircraft procurement to modernize existing units be authorized into the 1960's while pressing for the most rapid development of operational intermediate Range and Inter-Continental Ballistic Missiles.

b). The SAC base structure be made less vulnerable to surprise attack through dispersion and other protective measures.

c). An accelerated research and development support be provided for such key programs as missiles.

d). Additional troop transport be authorized in the form both of modern aircraft and ships.

e). The program of equipping both surface and underwater ships with missiles of various types be accelerated and additional funds for anti-submarine defense be provided.

f). Military pay scales be raised to retain skilled officers and men.

34. Eisenhower, *Waging Peace*, p. 226.

35. Quoted in John Gittings, *Survey of the Sino-Soviet Dispute, 1963–1967* (London: Oxford University Press, 1968), p. 82.

36. I analyze this process in some detail in *The Diffusion of Power* (New York: Macmillan, 1972), pp. 28–35.

37. Arnold L. Horelick and Myron Rush, *Strategic Power and Soviet Foreign Policy* (Chicago: University of Chicago Press, 1966), p. 35.

38. "Department of Defense Statement on U.S. Military Strength," April 14, 1964.

39. Quoted in Horelick and Rush, *Strategic Power*, p. 64.

40. Ibid.

41. Eisenhower, *Waging Peace*, pp. 206–209.

42. Robert S. Rosholt et al., *An Administrative History of NASA, 1958–1963* (Washington, D.C.: NASA, 1966), Chapter 1, pp. 4–5, and relevant footnotes.

43. Letter from Nikolai A. Bulganin to President Eisenhower, September 19, 1955, Department of State *Bulletin* 33, no. 852, October 24, 1955, p. 645; and letter from Premier Bulganin to President Eisenhower, February 1, 1956, Department of State *Bulletin* 34, no. 874, March 26, 1956, p. 517.

44. Text supplied by Mr. Katz.

45. F. M. Cornford, *Microcosmographia Academica* (Cambridge, Eng.: Bowes and Bowes, 1933), preface to third edition.

46. In a discussion of this matter while the text was being drafted, Robert Bowie suggested that satellite photography, reflecting

the emergence of a new impersonal technology, was easier for the Soviet Union to accept than manned flight in aircraft, the latter carrying with it more of the flavor of conventional espionage. Ted Carpenter added the observation that U-2 flights, by violating airspace, violated existing international law, whereas no law existed with respect to outer space. And, as Khrushchev acknowledged to de Gaulle in April 1960 (p. 11, above), the Soviet decision to launch its first Sputnik, freely overflying other nations, made the acceptance of satellite photography inevitable.

47. Morrow interview. Clark Clifford, an authoritative source on this matter, recalled in a conversation of January 23, 1982, that the idea for Point Four did, indeed, derive from an official of modest status in the State Department. Clifford does not recall whether he served on Latin American affairs under Rockefeller. Acheson did not oppose the idea, as is generally believed, but fought and won a battle to have the Point Four program administered within the State Department rather than by the separate agency Clifford would have preferred.

48. Gerard C. Smith Oral History Interview, Philip A. Crowl, interviewer, October 13, 1965, John Foster Dulles Oral History Project, Princeton University Library, transcript, p. 108.

49. See *Europe after Stalin* (Austin: University of Texas Press, 1981), p. 82. The thoughtful comments of John W. Hanes, Jr., a close aide of Dulles, on the tension between Dulles and Rockefeller deserve quotation. They are drawn from a letter to me of August 3, 1981, responding to an earlier draft of this book.

I believe your analysis both of the fact of, and the reasons for, the inherent problem between a Secretary of State and a principal presidential advisor on foreign policy is unchallengeable. I do not myself, however, find this as troubling as you seem to. I would venture to guess that Mr. Eisenhower (among others) also did not find it particularly troubling (which is quite a different thing than finding it occasionally irritating).

I doubt that, at the highest levels of policy (whether in or out of government), complete harmony is a useful servant of the principal decision maker. As in all other matters, of course, this statement must be accepted with a dictum of moderation. There is obviously a point at which disharmony becomes disruption and chaos.

Also, the roles which individuals play (and you perceptively describe the differing roles of the Secretary of State and the presidential advisor) usually both define and constrict (or, at times, perhaps expand) the ideas and concepts that individuals have. Perhaps it is more accurate to say that such roles direct the amount of time and thought that individuals may give to "thinking" (and about what) as opposed to "doing" what must be done day by day; and also require a decent (which is substantial) support of the ideas and views of those they lead within an organization if the organization is to function effectively, and loyally.

In this regard, one cannot read John Foster Dulles' books, written long before he was Secretary of State, without realizing that this pillar of the establishment profoundly understood the inevitability and the importance of change, as well as the usefulness of its disruptions. The very titles of his books underline this. And yet the Secretary of State, for the reasons you set forth, must maintain an ongoing operational department which cannot constantly be convulsed by change. . . .

And yet the Secretary of State understood well the formidable difficulties (also well known to you) of achieving any true meshing or meaningful stimulation between a person or group of persons engaged in long range thinking (and therefore able only somewhat superficially to keep abreast of the day to day crises), and those engaged in handling those same daily requirements of foreign policy and diplomacy. (Perhaps these problems are less at the Department of Defense, where presumably they are not engaged in actually fighting battles every day—I don't know.)

The various heads of his policy planning staff, with all their personal closeness to, access to and support by Secretary Dulles, had not less than the usual number of complaints common to all heads of the policy planning staff: that they didn't get sufficient audience for their long range views, and that they couldn't get them suitably inserted into current operational policy. . . . [The author of this book, who directed the Policy Planning Council in the period 1961–1966, must report that he had no cause for complaint on this score.]

Reverting to my first point, you note that Mr. Dulles, in the end, applauded the open skies initiative for its important result as to the role of the President on the international stage, and, therefore, of the United States. I doubt that this was, in any way, a grudging recognition. More likely, I think, it was a natural reaction when, finally, he looked at the entire matter from his own personal perspective, as opposed to looking at it as Secretary of State (and therefore often through the eyes of others within the Department advising and commenting to him). Indeed, if you will permit a wild leap of imagination, I would have found nothing inconsistent with Mr. Dulles having originated and pushed such a proposal through the bureaucracy had his role been that occupied by Nelson Rockefeller. (It is an intriguing thought as to what Nelson's reaction might have been had he been sitting over in Foggy Bottom at the same time.)

50. William B. Macomber Oral History Interview, Philip A. Crowl, interviewer, January 19, 1966, John Foster Dulles Oral History Project, Princeton University Library, transcript, p. 112.

51. The unity of the period from the launching of the first Sputnik to the Cuban missile crisis is tracked out in my *Diffusion of Power*, especially pp. 251–253.

52. For an analysis of this conference in relation to the resumption of Hanoi's insurrectional activities in South Vietnam, see ibid., pp. 40–49.

53. Eisenhower, *Mandate for Change*, p. 131.

54. Eisenhower draws on a passage from this speech to open Book 3 of his *Waging Peace*, p. 237.

Index

Center of International Studies, 27
Central Intelligence Agency
(CIA), 3, 90, 122
Childs, Marquis, 195n
China, Nationalist, 188
China, People's Republic of, 196n;
agriculture of, 155; and Asia,
157, 172; and Cold War, 157;
and developing countries, 156;
first Five-Year Plan of, 15; and
Geneva summit, 187–188; and
Indochina, 23, 97; and Korean
War, 15, 23; and U.S., 56, 188;
and U.S.S.R., 14, 23, 81, 96–97,
172; and Vietnam, 97
Churchill, Winston S., 14, 24
Clifford, Clark M., 87, 203n
Cocom Committee, 187
Cold War, 29, 39–40, 91, 155–
158, 173, 178
Columbia University, 27
COMECON, 22
Cominform, 186
Communism, 14, 58, 73–74, 96–
97, 186–187
Congo, 73–74, 97
Cornford, F. M., 82, 202n
Council of Foreign Ministers, 23–
24, 49, 63, 65–66, 78, 113, 185
Council on Foreign Relations, 65,
69
Crowl, Philip A., 203n, 205n
Cuba, 78, 95–98, 205n
Czechoslovakia, 172, 178

Defense Department, 91, 202n,
204n; and Anderson, 3, 38–39;
and Atoms for Peace proposal,
62; and mutual aerial inspection,
30, 124, 132; and Quantico I
Panel, 30, 34, 123–124, 132;
and Quantico II Panel, 200n; and
Rockefeller, 38–39, 100; and
Rockefeller Panel, 71; and Rostow, 30; and Speier, 124; and
State Department, 90

de Gaulle, Charles, 11, 203n
Democratic party (U.S.), 57, 156,
195n
Desmond, James, 65–66, 198n
developing countries, 97, 102, 141,
143; and China, 156; and U.S.,
12–13, 30, 65, 73, 100, 156,
171–172, 176, 181–183; and
U.S.S.R., 15, 22, 30, 65, 73, 100;
and Western Europe, 65
diffusion of power, 100, 102–103,
176, 205n
disarmament, 127; and aerial photography, 6, 9, 60, 79–81, 83–
84, 104–105; and Atoms for
Peace proposal, 38, 62–63, 186;
banning of nuclear weapons,
137–138, 142, 144, 187; budgetary control plan, 137, 142,
144; and Bulganin, 79–80, 128;
and conventional forces, 137;
and Council of Foreign Ministers, 63; demobilization, 137–
138; and developing countries,
172, 176, 182–183; and Dulles,
105, 128, 130–131, 135, 197n–
198n; and Eden, 107, 112–113,
128; and Eisenhower, 3–12,
29–32, 34–36, 40, 45–47,
51–52, 54, 57–58, 60, 62–
63, 84, 102, 104–105, 107,
109–113, 128, 130–131,
133–146, 174–175, 179,
182–183, 197n; and Geneva
summit, 3–9, 29–32, 34–36,
40, 45, 47, 51–52, 54, 57–58,
60, 62–63, 79–80, 84, 104–
105, 109–113, 128, 130–146,
174–176, 178–183, 186, 198n;
and Germany, 137, 181, 185;
graduated, 29, 32, 132–133; and
higher standard of life, 141,
143–144, 172; and inspection,
4–9, 12, 19–20, 23, 29–32,
34–36, 40, 45–47, 51–54,
56–57, 60, 62–63, 79–81,

proposal, 3–12, 29, 34–36, 40, 45–47, 50–52, 54, 56–63, 78–79, 84, 87, 102, 104–109, 111, 113, 126–128, 130–131, 133–146, 169–184, 198n, 205n; and Paris summit, 11; and psychological warfare, 37–38, 57, 59–60, 78, 186; and Quantico I Panel, 12–13, 26, 29, 34, 36–38, 40, 44–45, 98, 120, 122, 125–127, 130, 165–166; and Quantico II Panel, 13, 65, 67, 95, 98; and Radford, 3, 36, 50, 55, 61, 104, 106, 136; and rearmament, 109–110, 141, 143; and Rockefeller, 3–5, 13, 25–26, 34–47, 49–52, 54, 56, 58, 61, 65, 67, 70–71, 84, 87–88, 91, 95, 99, 104, 107, 120, 125, 128, 130–131, 133–136, 165, 169–184; and Rostow, 47, 51–52, 158, 169–183; and satellite reconnaissance, 11; and Second World War, 88, 109, 141, 143; and Sputnik, 76, 97; and Stassen, 3–5, 35–36, 39–40, 48, 50, 56, 61, 104–107, 109–112, 128, 130–131, 133, 135–136, 184; and State Department, 39, 62, 127; and Strauss, 39, 62; and summit proposals, 14; and U.K., 3–4, 7, 14, 36, 59, 107–108, 112–113, 128, 135; and U.N., 38, 102–103, 111, 125, 139, 142, 145; and unilateral aerial reconnaissance, 10–11, 193n; and U.S. intelligence, 108, 113, 134; and U.S. space program, 76, 98–99; and U.S.S.R., 3–4, 6–12, 29, 46–48, 57–58, 60, 62–63, 76, 78–79, 86, 97–99, 102, 104–105, 108, 112–113, 126, 128, 134–135, 145, 160–161, 163, 172–175, 178–180, 187, 193n

European Defense Community (EDC), 24, 162

Far East, 172, 188
Faure, Edgar, 3, 7, 57, 128, 135
Ford, Gerald, 102
Foster, William, 70
France: and disarmament, 186; and EDC, 162; and Geneva summit, 3, 5, 7, 14, 24, 48–49, 57, 59, 61, 108, 125, 128, 135, 159, 163, 186; and Germany, 24, 159, 188, 197n; and NATO, 24; and Open Skies proposal, 5, 7, 57, 108, 128, 135; and Paris summit, 11; and Suez crisis, 73; and U.K., 24, 73, 108, 197n; and U.N., 186; and U.S., 11, 24, 48–49, 57, 59, 61, 76, 108, 124–125, 128, 135, 159, 163, 188, 197n; and U.S.S.R., 11, 24, 76, 159, 188, 197n
Free, Lloyd, 87, 127

Gaither Report, 70
Geneva summit conference: and D. Anderson, 36, 104, 106, 108–109, 112–113; and R. Anderson, 50, 52, 54–55, 104–106, 109, 127–128, 135–136, 197n; and Atoms for Peace proposal, 186; and Bohlen, 63, 198n; and Bulganin, 60, 63, 79, 128, 187; and Canada, 186; and China, 187–188; and Council of Foreign Ministers, 185; and developing countries, 175–176, 181–182; and disarmament, 3–9, 29–32, 34–36, 40, 45, 47–48, 51–52, 54, 56–58, 60, 62–63, 79, 84, 87, 104–106, 109–113, 128, 130–146, 172, 174–176, 178–182, 186–187, 197n–198n; and division of Europe, 172, 178, 181, 186–187; and Dulles, 3, 5, 7, 9, 24, 34–38, 40, 45, 47–51, 54, 58–59, 84, 87, 104–106, 109, 112–113, 126–128, 131, 135, 159, 160–164, 169–183, 185, 189n, 195n,

197n–198n; and Eden, 24, 36, 55, 108, 112–113, 126, 128, 159, 162; and Eisenhower, 3–12, 24–26, 29, 34–38, 40, 45, 47–52, 54–63, 78–79, 84, 87, 104–106, 108–113, 122, 125–128, 130–131, 133–146, 158, 160–161, 163, 169–184, 187, 195n, 197n; and Europe, 174; and France, 3, 14, 24, 48–49, 57, 59, 61, 105, 108, 125, 128, 135, 159, 163, 186, 188, 197n; and Free, 127; and George, 24, 109; and Germany, 12, 24, 29, 31–32, 51–52, 61, 137, 159, 174, 179–182, 185, 187–188, 197n; and Goodpaster, 54–56, 104, 106, 109, 127, 136; and Gruenther, 36, 55, 104–106, 108, 128, 198n; and inspection, 4–12, 29–32, 34–36, 40, 45, 47, 50–52, 54–63, 79, 87, 104–106, 109–113, 124, 130–146, 169–184, 198n; and Jackson, 125, 159–164; and Johnson, 57–58; and Khrushchev, 21, 63, 80, 187; and Kintner, 54, 127, 197n; and Macmillan, 112, 162; and Merchant, 36, 106, 189n; and Millikan, 158; and Molotov, 126, 186; and NATO, 105, 185, 187; and Open Skies proposal, 3–12, 29–32, 34–63, 78–79, 84, 87, 104–106, 108–113, 124–146, 169–184, 189n, 197n–198n; and Parker, 45, 54, 127, 130; and Pettee, 50; and Possony, 50, 52, 54, 127, 197n; and Quantico I Panel, 11–12, 26–34, 36–38, 40, 45, 51, 56, 65, 120–122, 124, 126–128, 130–133; and Radford, 36, 50, 52, 54–55, 61, 104, 106, 127–128, 135–136, 197n–198n; and Reston, 58–62, 197n–198n; and Rockefeller,

3–5, 7, 11–12, 25–26, 34–38, 40, 45, 47, 49–52, 54–56, 58, 61, 65, 84, 87, 104, 120, 127–128, 130–131, 133–136, 169–184, 197n; and Rostow, 51–52, 120, 125, 127, 157–158, 169–183; and Stassen, 35–36, 48, 50, 54–56, 61, 104–106, 112, 127–128, 130–131, 133, 135–136, 184; and State Department, 94, 120, 127–128, 185–188; and U.K., 3–4, 14, 24, 48–49, 55, 59, 61, 105, 108, 112–113, 125–126, 128, 135, 159–160, 162–163, 186, 197n; and U.N., 186; and U.S., 3–14, 20–21, 23–26, 29–37, 40, 45, 48–52, 54–63, 65, 78–79, 84, 104–105, 108–113, 120–121, 125–146, 156–164, 169–188, 195n, 197n–198n; and U.S.S.R., 3, 6–9, 12, 14, 20, 24, 29, 31–32, 48–49, 59–60, 63, 65, 72, 78–79, 84, 104–105, 108, 112–113, 126, 128, 130–132, 134, 136, 157, 159–161, 163, 173–175, 178–180, 185–188, 189n, 197n; and Warsaw Pact, 185; and Zhukov, 126, 163
George, Walter, 24, 39, 109
Germany, 18, 23; and Council of Foreign Ministers, 65, 185; and disarmament, 107, 137, 181, 185; division of, 107, 113, 179, 181; elections in, 32, 51, 180; and France, 24, 159, 188, 197n; and Geneva summit, 12, 24, 29, 31–32, 47, 51–52, 61, 113, 137, 174, 179–182, 185, 198n; and NATO, 24, 185; neutralism in, 188; and Open Skies proposal, 107; rearmament of, 24, 124, 159, 187; rocketry of, 16; and U.K., 24, 197n; unity of, 12, 29, 32, 61, 137, 159, 174, 181; and

Nixon, Richard M., 72, 99
North Atlantic Treaty Organization
(NATO), 22, 73, 196n; and Berlin,
99; and France, 24, 105; and
G.D.R., 55; and Geneva summit,
185; and Germany, 24, 185; and
Gruenther, 3, 55; and nuclear
weapons, 71; and Open Skies
proposal, 55, 105; and Potsdam
teams, 55, 107; and U.K., 24,
205; and U.S., 8, 24, 29, 71, 99,
101, 105, 107, 151, 178, 187;
and U.S.S.R., 8, 24, 29, 99, 105,
187; and Warsaw Pact, 29, 55,
107, 185
Norway, 76
nuclear delivery systems: and
ATLAS, 10; development of, 10,
15–19; and Germany, 16; inter-
mediate-range missiles, 16–19,
75, 96, 201n; lags in capability,
19, 73–76, 80, 82–83; long-
range missiles, 16–19; strategic
air commands, 17–19; sub-
marine missiles, 19; and THOR,
10; and U.S., 10, 16–19, 76–77,
83, 96, 156; and U.S.S.R., 16–19,
73–77, 80, 83, 96, 156; and V-2,
16
nuclear weapons, 176, 182; air defense against, 18–19, 156; and
civil defense, 70, 131; and delivery systems, 16–19, 73–77, 80,
82–83, 96, 156, 201n; and deterrent policy, 52, 65, 70–71,
96, 98; development of, 15–17,
20, 23, 62, 109; and fear of nuclear war, 11–12, 16, 18, 52,
57–58, 62, 79, 109–110, 115,
127, 131, 140–141, 145, 180,
196n; and gaps, 11–13, 15–16,
20, 29, 76, 83; and NATO, 71; and
nuclear blackmail, 11, 96; and
parity, 12; and peaceful uses of
nuclear energy, 115; and retalia-
tion, 18, 71; and testing, 15, 83;

and U.S., 6, 9, 11–13, 15–16,
18, 29, 62, 76, 156, 201n; and
U.S.S.R., 6, 9, 11–13, 15–18, 20,
23, 29, 60, 76, 156

O'Connor, Rodney, 43
oil supplies, 101, 150
Open Skies proposal, 91, 95, 100;
aftermath of, 57–84, 128, 184;
and D. Anderson, 3–4, 35–36,
104, 106–109, 112–113; and R.
Anderson, 3, 5, 50, 52, 54–55,
104–106, 109, 128, 135–136,
197n; and Brownjohn, 36, 55;
and Bulganin, 63, 79–80, 128;
and Council of Foreign Ministers, 63; and Defense Department, 30, 34, 124, 132, 135;
and disarmament, 102, 104–
105, 107, 109, 111–113,
122–123, 128, 130–146,
169–183; and Dulles, 3, 5, 7,
9–10, 34–36, 40, 45–47,
50–51, 54–55, 58, 62, 92,
104–106, 109, 112, 127–128,
130–131, 135–136, 169–183,
198n, 205n; and Eden, 4, 7, 36,
55, 107–108, 112–113, 128;
and Eisenhower, 3–12, 29,
34–36, 40, 45–47, 50–52,
54–63, 78–80, 84, 102, 104–
109, 111–113, 124, 126, 128,
130–131, 133–146, 169–184,
198n, 205n; and France, 5, 7, 57,
105, 108, 128, 135; and F.R.G.,
107–108; and G.D.R., 107–
108; and Geneva summit, 3–6,
34–56, 104–113, 122–146,
169–183, 189n, 197n–198n;
and Germany, 107; and Goodpaster, 3–4, 10, 35, 54–56, 104,
106–107, 109, 127, 136; and
Gruenther, 3, 5, 36, 55, 104,
106–107, 128, 198n; and Jackson, 120–128; and Johnson,
57–58; and Khrushchev, 8–10,

27, 196n; and Eisenhower, 12–13, 26–27, 34, 36–38, 40, 44–45, 51, 98, 120, 122, 124–125, 130, 165–166; and Geneva summit, 26–34, 36, 38, 40, 45, 51, 56, 65, 79, 120–121, 124, 127–128, 130–133; and Goodpaster, 27, 32, 56; and Hoover, 120; and inspection, 11, 29–34, 36, 40, 45, 51, 56, 79, 122–124, 130–133, 155; and Jackson, 27–28, 30, 32, 44–45, 51, 120–128, 165–166; and Johnson, 27–29, 121, 147–154, 196n; and Kintner, 26, 37, 121; and Linebarger, 27, 196n; and Millikan, 27, 30, 124; and Mosely, 27; and NATO, 124, 196n; and Open Skies proposal, 11–12, 29–34, 36, 40, 45, 51, 56, 79, 92, 122–124, 127–128, 130–133, 165–166; organization of, 26–27, 120–122; and Parker, 27, 34, 37, 45, 130; and Pettee, 27, 50, 196n; and Possony, 27, 30, 124, 196n; and psychological warfare, 37–38, 124; report of, 28, 30–34, 40, 44, 98, 122–124, 130–133, 147–154, 157, 165–166; and Rockefeller, 11–12, 26–27, 31–34, 36–38, 40–41, 44–45, 51, 56, 120–121, 124–125, 127, 130, 155, 165–166; and Rostow, 27–33, 51, 120–122, 147, 155–158, 196n; and Shockley survey, 147; and Speier, 27, 30, 124; and Stassen, 27, 32, 34–35, 127, 130; and State Department, 27, 32, 34, 40, 92, 120–122, 124; and U.S.S.R., 123–124, 130–132, 147–154, 196n; and U.S. test of U.S.S.R. intentions, 12–13, 26–27, 34, 36–38, 40, 44–45, 51, 65, 79, 132

Quantico II Panel, 100; and Council of Foreign Ministers, 65–66; and Desmond, 65–66; and developing countries, 13, 98; and Eisenhower, 12–13, 65, 68, 95, 98; and increased military spending, 12–13, 66–68, 97–98, 199n, 201n–202n; and Kennedy, 66, 68; and Kissinger, 68; and limited warfare, 66, 199n; and Millikan, 66; and nuclear war, 199n; organization of, 65, 67; recommendations of, 66–68, 98, 200n–202n; and Rockefeller, 12, 65–68, 95; and Rostow, 66–67; and State Department, 66; and U.N., 201n; and U.S., 12, 65–68, 98, 199n

Quemoy, 73

Radford, Arthur W., 105; and Anderson, 54–55, 104, 106, 127–128, 135–136, 197n; and Dulles, 35–36, 54, 104, 106, 127, 135–136, 198n; and Eden, 128; and Eisenhower, 50 55, 61, 104, 106, 136; and Geneva summit, 3, 5, 10, 35–36, 50, 52–55, 61, 104, 106, 127–128, 136, 197n–198n; and Gruenther, 36, 55, 104, 106, 128, 198n; and inspection, 35–36, 52–54, 61–62, 104, 106; and Open Skies proposal, 3, 5, 10, 35–36, 52–55, 61–62, 104, 106, 127–128, 136, 197n–198n; and Possony, 52–53, 127, 197n; and Rockefeller, 35–36, 52, 61, 104, 107, 127, 197n; and Stassen, 35–36, 61, 104, 106, 127, 136

Randall, Clarence, 39

RAND Corporation, 27, 30, 81, 124, 189n, 193n

Repplier, Theodore, 41–42

Republican party (U.S.), 57–58, 156

Reston, James, 58–62, 197n–198n

Richards, James, 39, 109
Robertson, Walter, 126
Rockefeller, Nelson A.: and Adams, 39–43; and Defense Department, 38–39, 100; and disarmament, 3–5, 7, 35–36, 40, 45–47, 52, 54–56, 58, 104, 106–107, 128–131, 133–136, 155, 169–183; and Dulles, 35–46, 49–51, 58, 67, 84–85, 87–88, 95, 104, 106–107, 120, 125, 128, 130–131, 135–136, 165–166, 169–183, 205n; and Eisenhower, 3–5, 7, 11, 13, 25–26, 34–47, 49–52, 54–56, 58, 61, 65, 67, 84, 87–88, 99, 104, 106–107, 120, 125–126, 128, 130–131, 133–136, 165–166, 169–184; and Geneva summit, 3–5, 7, 25–26, 34–38, 40, 45, 47, 49–52, 54–56, 58, 61, 65, 84, 87, 104, 120, 126–128, 130–131, 133–136, 169–184, 197n; and Hoover, 26, 43, 67, 120; and Jackson, 26, 38, 40, 42, 44, 121, 125–127; and Kintner, 26, 121, 127, 197n; and mutual inspection, 4–5, 7, 11, 34–36, 40, 45–47, 50–52, 54–56, 58, 61, 104, 106–107, 127–128, 130–131, 133–135, 155, 169–184; and NSC, 45, 77, 128–131, 133; and Open Skies proposal, 3–5, 7, 11, 34–36, 40, 45–47, 50–52, 54–56, 58, 61, 87, 104, 106–107, 127–128, 130–131, 133–136, 169–184, 197n; and Operations Coordinating Board, 26, 37; and Parker, 26, 127, 129–131; as presidential aide, 26–27, 36–37, 39–46, 66–67, 84–85, 87–88, 205n; and psychological warfare, 26, 35, 38; and Quantico I Panel, 11–12, 26–27, 31–34, 36–38, 40–41, 44–45, 51, 56, 120–

121, 124–125, 127, 130, 155, 165–166; and Quantico II Panel, 12, 65–67, 95; and Radford, 35–36, 50, 52, 104, 106–107, 127, 136, 197n; and Rockefeller Panel, 13, 67; and Rostow, 27, 31, 50–51, 66–67, 120, 126, 155–158, 169–183; and Stassen, 5, 35–36, 45, 50, 52, 55–56, 104, 106–107, 127–128, 130–131, 133, 135–136, 184; and State Department, 38–40, 85, 128
Rockefeller Panels, 13, 67–68, 70–71, 199n
rocketry, development of, 9–10, 15–19
Roosevelt, Franklin D., 39, 94
Rosholt, Robert S., 202n
Rostow, W. W., 54, 95, 193n–194n, 202n; and arms race, 51, 155–158; and Asia, 156–157, 175, 196n; and China, 155–157; and Cold War, 155–158; and Cuba, 205n; and Defense Department, 30; and developing countries, 99, 156–157; and disarmament, 47, 51–52, 122, 155; and Dulles, 169–183; and Eisenhower, 47, 51–52, 125, 127, 158, 169–183; and Geneva summit, 31, 51–52, 120, 157–158, 169–183; and Germany, 51–52; and inspection, 30, 47, 51, 81, 83, 122, 155; and Jackson, 121, 126; and Japan, 156; and Johnson, 95; and Kennedy, 95; and Millikan, 158; and Open Skies proposal, 122, 157; and Policy Planning Council, 95, 205n; as presidential aide, 95; and Pugwash meeting, 81, 83; and Quantico I Panel, 27–33, 51, 120–121, 126, 155, 157, 196n; and Quantico II Panel, 66–67; and Rockefeller, 27, 31, 47, 50–51, 66–

78–80, 84, 102, 105, 108, 113, 123, 126, 132, 134–136, 145, 189n, 194n, 197n; and Paris summit, 10–11, 73; and Poland, 172, 178; and post-Stalin leadership, 14–15, 20–21, 86, 124, 156; postwar expansionism of, 14, 22; and Quemoy, 73; rocketry of, 18; and Rumania, 172, 178; and satellite reconnaissance, 10–12, 65, 81, 83, 194n, 203n; science and technology of, 17–18, 29, 150–151, 154; and Second World War, 18, 20; and Southeast Asia, 101; and Sputnik, 10, 13, 29, 68–69, 71, 73–77, 80, 97–98, 203n; strategic air command of, 17–19; transport of, 156; and U.K., 21, 23–24, 76, 105, 197n; and U.N., 23–24, 114–119, 186; and U.S., 3–20, 22–24, 26, 29–32, 37–38, 46–49, 53, 57–60, 62–63, 65–66, 68–81, 83, 95, 97–102, 105, 108, 113–114, 121–122, 124, 127–128, 131–132, 134–136, 145, 147–161, 163, 172–175, 178–180, 187–188, 189n–194n, 201n, 203n; and U-2, 10–11, 73–75, 80–82, 193n, 203n; and Warsaw Pact, 29, 107; and Western Europe, 15, 22–23, 65, 74–76, 113; world strategy of, 15, 19–20, 22–23, 31, 59, 78; and Yugoslavia, 14, 186
United Nations (U.N.), 19–20, 23, 125; charter of, 24, 187, 201n; Disarmament Commission of, 4, 7, 63, 111, 118–119, 139, 142, 145, 186; General Assembly of, 89, 102, 114–119; and Open Skies proposal, 63, 111; and U.S., 38, 63, 111, 118–119, 139, 142, 145, 172, 186–187; and U.S.S.R., 23–24, 114–119, 186
United States (U.S.): and Afghan-

istan, 101; and Africa, 101, 175, 181; aircraft of, 149–150, 152; armor of, 148–150, 153–154; and arms race, 11–13, 15–18, 20, 29, 31, 51, 62, 70–77, 83, 98, 102, 109, 121, 132, 155, 157–158, 160–161, 172–173, 178–180, 182, 196n; and Asia, 47, 156–157, 175, 196n; and Atoms for Peace proposal, 38, 62, 172, 186; and Austria, 24; and Berlin, 73, 101; budget of, 12–13, 20, 31, 66–68, 71, 97–101, 156, 171, 199n; and Burma, 156; and the Caribbean, 101; and Castro, 73; and China, 26, 156–157, 188, 196n; and Cold War, 155–158, 173, 178; and the Congo, 73, 97; and Congress, 24, 57–58, 60, 72, 97, 124, 161, 195n; conventional military forces of, 29, 66, 99; and Council of Foreign Ministers, 63, 65–66; and Cuba, 78, 97–98; and developing countries, 12–13, 30, 65, 72, 97–100, 102, 156, 171–172, 176, 181–183; and diffusion of power, 102–103, 176, 182, 205n; and disarmament, 3–9, 16, 29–32, 34–36, 40, 45–48, 50–58, 60, 62–63, 79–84, 102–105, 107, 109–114, 118–119, 122–123, 128–146, 172, 174–183, 186–187, 197n–198n, 201n; and division of Europe, 172, 178, 181, 186; and Eastern Europe, 113, 174, 186; economy of, 20, 72, 98, 102, 156, 171; and Egypt, 22, 72–73, 97; electronics in, 148, 150, 154; engineering in, 29, 121; and exchange of military information, 57, 60–62, 79, 105, 135, 145; foreign aid of, 99, 101, 171, 178; foreign policy of, 12–13, 66, 68–72, 85, 88, 92–95, 98–102,

Vanguard missiles, 77
Vietnam, 15, 96–97, 205n
V-2 rockets, 16

Wadsworth, James J., 118–119
Warsaw Pact, 29, 55, 107, 185
Washburn, Abbott, 124–125
Washington, George, 160
Washington Post, 58
Western Europe, 196n; and developing countries, 65; and disarmament, 127; and Geneva summit, 23, 181; and Germany, 23; and U.S., 14, 65, 72, 76, 113, 127, 156, 178–181; and U.S.S.R., 15, 22–23, 65, 74–76, 113
Western European Union, 24
Whitman, Ann, 37–39, 63, 104, 112, 185, 196n
Wilson, Charles, 67
Wilson, Woodrow, 39
Wisner, Frank, 120
Worthman, Paul, 74, 189n–194n

Yugoslavia, 14, 186

Zhukov, Georgi K., 126, 163

Lightning Source UK Ltd.
Milton Keynes UK
UKHW010045211221
396012UK00001B/15

9 780292 760240